No One Saw My Pain

Why Teens Kill Themselves

No One Saw My Pain

Why Teens Kill Themselves

ANDREW E. SLABY, M.D.

LILI FRANK GARFINKEL

W·W· NORTON & COMPANY

NEW YORK   LONDON

Printed in the United States of America

First published as a Norton paperback 1996

The text of this book is composed in Palatino
with the display set in Spartan
Composition and manufacturing by the Maple–Vail Book Manufacturing Group.
Book design by R. Mandel

Library of Congress Cataloging-in-Publication Data

Slaby, Andrew E.
    No one saw my pain : why teens kill themselves /
Andrew E. Slaby, Lili Frank Garfinkel.
        p. cm.
    Includes bilbiographical references.
    1. Teenagers—Suicidal behavior—Case studies. 2. Depression
in adolescence—Case studies. I. Garfinkel, Lili. II. Title.
RJ506.S9G37   1994
616.85′8445′00835—dc20   93-28398

ISBN 0-393-31392-1

W. W. Norton & Company, Inc., 500 Fifth Avenue, New York, N.Y. 10110
W. W. Norton & Company Ltd., 10 Coptic Street, London WC1A 1PU

3 4 5 6 7 8 9 0

TO THE FAMILIES OF

CHAD, CARLY, JOHN, DAVID,
TIM, BRET, SARAH, AND KENT

*WITHOUT THEIR COURAGE, COMPASSION, AND
WILLINGNESS TO SHARE THEIR EXPERIENCES WITH
US, THIS BOOK WOULD NOT HAVE BEEN POSSIBLE.*

TO BARRY

*WITHOUT HIS GUIDANCE, ENCOURAGEMENT, AND LOVE
FOR HIS WORK THIS BOOK COULD NEVER HAVE BEEN
WRITTEN.*

CONTENTS

PREFACE

Each of the personal stories in this book is based on an actual case of suicide or attempted suicide. Generally, only those details that could clearly identify the teens or their families have been altered. My journey with all these families has taught me a great deal, and I am indebted to them for allowing their stories to be shared. This book is dedicated to the memories of their children and to their courage in reliving what was undoubtedly the worst experience of their lives. Although all of the cases share some common threads, each has some unique features, particularly with regard to the distinctive disguises that may mask a diagnosis of depression and a teenager in crisis.

I have been interested in suicide in youth since 1972. My perspective has always been from the vantage point of a clinician treating depressed and suicidal teens. I recognized that effective treatment often required me to take a strong advocacy role: I had to explain to parents and teens how depression and self-destructiveness affected school, home, community, and athletic activities. To achieve this, I asked Lili Frank Garfinkel, with her background in developing resources in parent and child advocacy, to help me reframe clinical psychiatric concepts into community-based information for teachers, coaches, classmates, family members, and others who interact with profoundly troubled teens. She encouraged me to modify the clinical and research goals to include work with families experiencing bereavement resulting from having had a child commit suicide.

The unabated suffering that survivors conveyed was as compelling as the painful images of depressed teens.

I have learned many lessons from the families with whom I have worked over the years. Their words, thoughts, and actions are present in the chapters that follow. These are not hypothetical cases—they are real—and the conclusions and advice are presented in practical terms for parents, educators, counselors, and peers of depressed adolescents.

Regretfully, I have no cases pertaining to African-American youths. The suicide rate among African-American youth is about one-third to one-fifth that of Caucasian teens.[1] I have no doubt but that, because of a fragmented and unequal system of access to psychiatric care, minority youth have less professional contact with psychiatrists or psychologists, particularly in a university or private practice setting. Moreover, there is a general shortage of persons of color in the mental health profession and a concomitant perception among clients of color that psychiatry is ignorant of and insensitive to issues that have strong cultural and racial influences.

Mental health services for many African-American, Hispanic, and Asian youth, if available at all, are in large part channeled through the juvenile court system, state social welfare system and other public venues. Each of these services is burdened by large caseloads, a multiplicity of chronic and complex problems among the children and families they serve, few opportunities for staff training, a high staff turnover, and the likelihood that the staff in the "trenches" administering to the most difficult cases are the least experienced.

Obviously, our health-care system has not adequately responded to the needs of all children and teens in a proactive or preventive manner. We have certainly not served our youth well in concerns relating to mental health.

The cry of our title, *No One Saw My Pain*, comes from the many tragic accounts of depression and suicide I have heard. Even the word *pain* was chosen specifically to depict the extreme mental suffering resulting from depression and its most serious aftermath, suicide.

I wish to thank Dr. Barry Garfinkel, Associate Professor of Psychiatry at the University of Minnesota, for all of his work in helping to bring this book to fruition. The study of survivors of adolescent suicide was first conceptualized by Barry when he was Director of Research in Child and Adolescent Psychiatry at Brown University. Earlier he had worked with suicidal adolescents and their families while at the Hospital for Sick Children in Toronto; later he carried on this work in Minnesota. He has personally studied a number of the families described in disguised form in this volume and has inspired both myself and others interested in preventing adolescent and childhood suicide and in understanding how best to serve those who survive. My thanks to Barry for all he has done and for all he will continue to do for the community. He is a valued friend and colleague.

Andrew E. Slaby, M.D.

No One Saw My Pain

Why Teens Kill Themselves

One

TEENS IN PAIN

This book has been germinating for almost ten years. And in those ten years, psychiatry, particularly child and adolescent psychiatry, has gained twenty years in its scope of knowledge about diagnoses and treatment. In light of this progress, I would have hoped that a book about adolescent depression and suicide would never need to be written, that the suicide rate could be stemmed. On the contrary, the current statistics on youth suicide continue to be frightening. More than 5,000 youth under the age of twenty-five kill themselves in the United States every year. Of these, 2,000 are teenagers.[1] And for every completed suicide between 300 and 350 serious attempts are made.[2] Surveys have shown that as many as 60 percent of all high school students have thought about their own death or about killing themselves.[3] In addition, one out of every ten high school students experiences some form of severe depression during the high school years.[4]

I have counseled depressed teens and their families for the last twenty years. In that time I have made every effort to reach out to teachers, clergy, and counselors, as well as many other professionals concerned with the well-being of young people. My patients have included teens in crisis, young people preoccupied with morbid thoughts, teens who have made suicidal gestures or those who have actually attempted suicide, and most tragically, family members who have lost a teen to suicide. I feel tremendous relief and hope when I am able to intervene successfully with young people in crisis and their families. Whether I am directly involved in the therapeutic process or facilitate connection with other community resources, sparing as many people as possible the most severe consequences of depression remains my ongoing goal.

THE MENTAL PAIN OF DEPRESSION

Depression is commonly portrayed unidimensionally as profound, all-encompassing sadness. When I ask adults and teens how they would conceptualize a depressed person, they most often describe a hollow-eyed, miserable person who sleepwalks through life before taking an overdose. There is no understanding or recognition of the rage, the fear, and the insurmountable pain that are so much a part of depression. Imagine the worst physical pain you've ever had—a broken bone, a toothache, or labor pain—multiply it tenfold and take away the cause; then you can possibly approximate the pain of depression. The mental pain of depression is so all-consuming that it becomes impossible to derive any pleasure or satisfaction from life; no interests can stimulate attention and perseverance, no persons can adequately foster love or loyalty. The world is seen as bleak and gray. To someone who is profoundly depressed, the option of suicide becomes the only option, the only way to control life and end the unremitting pain.

Depression is a term that has been too loosely integrated into our vocabulary. When we say "I'm so depressed about . . ." and yet continue to function, work, play, interact with people, it means we're temporarily unhappy about something. Clinical depression, however, is not so transient. A diagnosis of depression is measurable according to specific characteristics, which include sleep disturbance (insomnia or sleeping all the time), changes in eating habits (overeating or lack of appetite), inability to concentrate, physical symptoms (such as headaches, stomachaches), agitation or fatigue, and wretched, morbid thoughts about oneself and the future.[5]

The pain of depression can be far more overwhelming, more incapacitating, than any physical pain. Individuals who are hurting emotionally think poorly of themselves and act in ways that will cause others to think poorly of them. As this cycle is perpetuated, they become more and more isolated and convinced of their worthlessness. It is understandable, then, that persons who are depressed engage in antisocial or delinquent behavior, develop unusually hostile relationships with those closest to them, or experience progressive difficulties with peer relationships. What they are really doing is creating in the minds of others the same negative impressions they already feel about themselves.

Options like reaching out and seeking help are rarely considered or are rejected outright, and as the depression evolves the only option that promises to shut off the pain is suicide.

THE IMPACT OF DEPRESSION

Clinical depression impacts people in real physiological as well as emotional ways. For a diagnosis of clinical depression to be made, it must last at least two weeks and include at least five of the following symptoms: the inability to concentrate, feelings of hopelessness, changes in regular eating habits, sleep disturbances, loss or lack of energy, behavioral changes (restlessness and agitation), engaging in risk-taking behaviors, changes in schoolwork and/or work habits, and thoughts of suicide. Often there is a decrease in sexual energy. In fact, depressed teens may turn to others through sexual encounters in order to gain some acceptance and positive feedback.

It is typical for people with depression to perceive life in an almost totally distorted and negative way, so that thinking and behavior become radically altered. Both one's past history and day-to-day life are rewritten and recast so that everything is seen in the bleakest terms.

It is estimated that approximately one in ten high school students can be diagnosed with depression at some time in his or her life. Many more are never identified. For some fortunate persons, an episode of clinical depression, even untreated, will pass without any lingering effects. For others, therapy and a course of antidepressant medication will be necessary. In either case, most teens who have depression do not go on to attempt or commit suicide. The pressing questions are: Can we determine which kids are more likely to attempt or commit suicide? What separates those people who live with depression from those who are preoccupied with thoughts about suicide, those who make specific plans to kill themselves, or those who actually carry out their plans or impulsively commit suicide?

Through "psychological autopsies" of teens who killed themselves or attempted to do so this book identifies those "markers" or features that predispose young people not only to depression but also to suicide. Some of these markers are: a family history of depression or suicide; learning disabilities (primarily because impulsivity is a quality common to both suicide and certain learning disabilities); a history of physical, sexual, or emotional abuse; delinquency; substance abuse; and recurrent, long-lasting episodes of depression.

At some time in our lives we all experience morbid thoughts, thoughts about our own death and the impact our death would have on those around us. Children begin to have these thoughts at an early age, usually around age four, and then again at different times as they mature. Usually these thoughts are transient and not likely to be associated with suicidal behavior. In rare cases, children might be preoccupied with thoughts of death and dying when a grandparent dies, even if a pet dies. They want to join the departed one in heaven. I have interviewed some very young children who have made primitive suicidal gestures for this reason.

Children and teenagers who experience depression at a young age may become dependent on others for affirmation of their very being. Instead of recognizing their own self-worth, they rely on others to provide them with positive feelings. They become needy, dependent, vulnerable teens and adults. Their pathway to help and healing is paved with missed cues and frustration.

Young persons who actually formulate a plan for their own suicide may not tell a soul of their plans, or they may swear a single trusted friend to secrecy about their intentions. Some teens even boast in a cavalier or indirect way about how they will one day kill themselves. They may give away treasured possessions; they may write unusually emotional letters to friends or an essay on suicide for English class. These behaviors should be viewed with alarm and clearly warrant immediate counseling and treatment.

When we talk about suicidal gestures, we are referring to attention-seeking behaviors, real cries for help. A suicidal gesture is a deliberate act of self-injury without the intention of dying. Gestures may include ingesting a nonlethal number of pills, self-injury such as minor wrist-slashing, or even waving a firearm around in front of friends. Teens who wave red flags in these ways may not want to die; yet, deaths have been known to occur in spite of the lack of intention.

Suicide attempts are really failed suicides. Some young persons are fortunate enough to be accidentally saved from killing themselves: They are found hanging, but alive, or survive a gunshot wound, or are revived from an overdose. The intent to kill themselves may persist, and they may try again, even succeed. On the other hand, some rescued teens view their survival as a sign that they were not meant to die, and with help they truly begin to work on dealing with their depression.

Any significant crisis related to depression, regardless of how it may manifest itself, should be viewed as a statement about the stresses in a young person's life, a lack of coping mechanisms, and/or society's response to his or her behaviors and problems at that time. The ultimate crisis precipitating the suicide attempt may reflect a breakdown at all three levels: stress and conflict, coping, and societal response.

Today, depression is better understood than ever before. It is a biological vulnerability that surfaces when sufficiently disturbing life experiences occur. It lies dormant in some individuals only to occur or recur when negative events come to bear on the vulnerable person. Depression alters the individual's functioning, creating additional problems. For instance, lacking the energy or desire to do constructive activities, the depressed teen frequently shows a deterioration in school and social functioning.

Adolescent depression is recognized, diagnosed, and treated more frequently than even five years ago. And yet the escalating statistics of adolescent suicide seem to nullify any serious progress. It is ironic that in an age where the cult of youth is so valued, emulated, and pursued, we have been unable to respond to our children and teens when they are in the greatest pain.

This generation of teens will have to learn and integrate—if they haven't already—a whole new system of strategies to cope with the complexity and variety of our societal and cultural norms. Whereas historically the family, the church, and the community frequently provided a safety net for children, where they were nurtured and sheltered and where certain types of behaviors were sanctioned and reinforced, this is no longer the case. Family breakdown, family and community violence, economic instability, stress, drugs—all are far too familiar to teens growing up today. And yet, these are still children, and developmentally they are not ready to face these formidable pressures. Ultimately, the crises that do confront many children who are depressed represent the convergence of complex stressors, immature and ineffectual coping mechanisms, and a lack of societal response.

DID NO ONE SEE THE PAIN?

It is hard to express the pain and poignancy I feel when meeting with families of children who have killed themselves. Whether we meet a week after the suicide or ten years later, I feel connected and bound by the need to help them understand what happened and go on with their lives. I am very aware that, no matter what insight I may help them discover, no matter what resolution or peace they may find in their lives, it will not be enough—they will struggle with guilt and with self-recriminations forever.

In nearly every case of suicide I have reviewed, clues to the adolescent's plans were overlooked or downplayed. They weren't intentionally missed, but unknowingly missed. This does not necessarily mean that the suicide could have been prevented. *Some people will kill themselves no matter what intervention takes place.* In my mind, many adolescent patients remain vulnerable; I worry and wonder how they will respond five or ten years from now, when a crisis may arise and other pressures and circumstances may influence their responses. The histories of many adults who have committed suicide include episodes of *me* severe depression, if not suicide attempts, during adolescence.

Why were the clues missed? Family members and friends did not understand the enormity of the changes they were seeing. They focused on the consequences and not on the underlying problem, so that "family problems" or "drug use" or "anorexia" became the diagnosis. Sometimes the anger, the confusion, and the irritability were treated, but not the depression. The underlying problem remained, torturous and festering.

Were their cries not heard? No, something was heard: Chad's silence, Sarah's continuous crying, Carly's rage, Tim's reactions to an abusive father, Kent's mental illness, David's drug use, and John's anxiety about his sexuality. Only in hindsight, however, do we realize that somehow the responses to their crises were not effective.

In the midst of a crisis, it is usually difficult to judge whether the choices that are made are the right ones, if the therapy is working, or if the medicine or counseling has helped. It is hard to stand back and say: Is this helping? If not, why? When the behaviors have not changed after a reasonable amount of time, some thought should be given to, at the very least, asking the treatment personnel some probing questions or seeking another opinion. Too often, parents are loath to ask these questions of professionals; they are intimidated and fear being blamed. Nevertheless, they must be assertive.

Among professionals there needs to be a greater understanding of the medical aspect of psychiatric illness that coexists with the psychological forces. Pediatricians, family doctors, internists, and emergency-room physicians must have more intensive training in treating depression. The same energy that we have brought to training students about AIDS and safe sex should be brought to providing knowledge about depression in all its guises. Drug abuse, risk-taking behaviors, promiscuity, and social isolation should provoke questions about suicidal thought and intentions. If we can save more young people it will be worth it.

Suicide is most often the fatal end point of depression, substance abuse, and delinquency. When one sees a pattern that often ends in suicide, immediate attention must be directed to the teen's safety. Hospitalization of the acutely suicidal adolescent is not optional; it cannot be postponed until tomorrow. The young person must be safe, and if the family cannot trust the child over the course of the day and night, then twenty-four-hour care in a hospital is mandatory. If an outpatient level of care is thought to be acceptable, the home must be made suicide-proof. This can never be completely accomplished; however, I ask parents to remove all firearms, dispose of all unused medicines, lock up the keys to the cars, and remove all ropes or cords that could be used for hanging. Making the method for self-destruction less accessible gives the teen more time to consider options other than suicide.

Treatment outside of the hospital most often involves three components: crisis intervention, counseling, and medication. Crisis intervention includes specific actions that adults can take to alleviate the immediate conflicts and problems facing the teenager. If it's a failing grade, work with the school to give an incomplete in the class. If it's parent-child conflict about a specific issue, address the disagreements in counseling. Problems need to be defused.

At one time counseling was synonymous with psychoanalytic therapy, which required a careful examination of the individual's past in order to gain insight into present behavior. Now we know that two types of counseling work best for depression— interpersonal and cognitive behavioral therapies. Interpersonal therapy examines and develops new ways of interacting with others so that fewer negative consequences occur when the depressed person interfaces with others. Cognitive behavioral therapy enables the client to acquire new verbal and mental strategies in self-directing current and future behaviors. Depressed teens don't have to fear facing their past alone to assure improvement. Today counseling is less disturbing and more practical than psychoanalysis.

Counseling addresses the behavioral and interactional problems resulting from the underlying depression. The most effective treatment, however, is a combination of medication and counseling. The original antidepressants had an array of side effects that made them very unpleasant to take. No longer do patients need to fear side effects such as constipation, blurred vision, lowered blood pressure, and dry mouth. The most recently developed antidepressants appear to be both safe and relatively free of side effects.

Patience is essential when the teen is taking an antidepressant. It may take one or two trials of different medicines to find the right one. It may take as long as four to six weeks for the teen to respond to the antidepressant. Moreover, the dose must be optimum. Probably two of the most common medication mistakes are giving too low a dose and giving it for an inadequate length of time.

Depression is a very treatable illness; the social, academic, and personal problems resulting from depression are much harder to alleviate. The painful stories that follow should reinforce our resolve to ensure proper treatment of all depressed and suicidal teens.

SILENCE: THE MIRROR OF DEPRESSION

Chad's family was referred to me by the family's minister, Reverend Howe. Chad Allen, age fifteen, had hung himself in his bedroom three months earlier. His death was the third suicide in his high school in eight months. The teens who killed themselves were not friends with one another. In any high school these events would have been considered frightening, but in the small town where Chad and his family lived it was enough to galvanize the community into action. Three weeks after Chad's funeral, I, along with several others, including Reverend Howe, spoke at a community-sponsored forum on suicide and depression in teens. Afterward, I spent some time with him, sharing different perspectives on the questions I had heard repeatedly from the audience: Why did these suicides happen here? Could they have been prevented? How was the profound sadness these young people were experiencing missed? I wanted to know more about the young people who had killed themselves; Reverend Howe was very open to providing me with the background he had.

"Drew," he said, "my contact with these kids was marginal, enough to say hi if I ran into them somewhere. Of the three families where kids committed suicide, Chad's parents, Gail and Ted, are the only ones who are members of our church. They weren't very involved or religious, and the night of Chad's death was the first time I had more than a passing conversation with them. Since Chad died, though, we've become very close. I learned that they had a rough time the last couple of years, and I've been counseling them. But it's complex. You see, they were separated for a while and got back together not long before Chad died. In fact, they were in family therapy, with an excellent and compassionate therapist, for a long time, so it's not like they didn't get help. I know you help families who have lost a child to suicide. Do you think you might have time to see them?"

I agreed to see them if they called and left Reverend Howe my phone number. Two weeks later Gail called to set up an appointment.

Both of Chad's parents came to the first meeting. Gail arrived half an hour early and paced the narrow hospital corridor outside the office, checking the clock repeatedly. I first noticed her when I completed the session with an earlier patient. She very quickly, almost imperceptibly, looked me over and then turned away. Ted arrived right on time and could barely contain his energy in his hearty handshake and ready smile. They took their seats in the office with some awkwardness, each making an obvious effort not to sit too close to me or face one another. I expressed my sympathy at their loss and explained to them that many families come here to share their child's story, and ultimately, I hope, find some peace.

"I hope that in our meetings you can come to understand the circumstances that led to Chad's death. I want to hear about you, about your life with Chad; if you'd like, we can think about including siblings, peers, teachers, or relatives in future sessions and get their input. Together, we'll try and reconstruct Chad's thoughts and behavior, so that you can better understand what went wrong. Most families find these meetings helpful; we will talk about your pain, the loss, the guilt, and hopefully we will arrive at some understanding about your child."

They both listened quietly. Gail was tall, dressed casually in jeans and a stylish sweater; she had delicate facial features, a ruddy complexion, no makeup, and hair tied back simply in a ponytail. She wore no jewelry except for an oversized watch, which she checked frequently during the long session. Her hands were large and rough, weather-beaten; they had seen hard physical labor, and seemed oddly disproportionate with the rest of her features.

By contrast, Ted looked as though he'd stepped out of a fashion magazine. I could sense him evaluating my clothing. Considerably shorter than his wife, tanned and carrying a slim leather briefcase, he exuded an aura of urgency and agitation. I noticed that when the phone on the desk flashed silently, his eyes searched the door. He clearly would have preferred to be elsewhere.

I was surprised when Gail, who had seemed very tentative and reluctant, quickly began: "I'd like to speak first because I'd been the custodial parent for the year before . . . before he died. I have a lot to say. Do I have a time limit?" I assured her that there was plenty of time. "Dr. Slaby, you may not be aware of this, but for a long time, Ted saw Chad only on weekends." Gail looked at Ted, saying, "I have to tell him everything." Turning back to me, she continued, "Chad was always a quiet kid, and gave us no problems until he turned thirteen. Until then, he seemed to like school, got C and B grades, nothing to get excited about, but we had no complaints. At first, I thought it was just typical adolescence; his body was changing, he had some acne, he seemed unhappy with his looks, his height, he was more down on his friends. He spent less and less time with us. After dinner he would go straight up to his room, listen to his tapes full blast, wouldn't talk much to us.

"I was working at a job where I had a lot of night meetings. Sometimes I would come home real late, and he was still listening to music, and sometimes I saw him writing in a notebook—I just assumed it was schoolwork. I never asked. After he died, we found the notebook. It was his journal." Gail looked up at me. "I'm sorry, I didn't even think to bring it today."

Gail took a deep breath, and then continued, "Right around then, Ted and I started to have problems. Ted had a drinking problem for a while, but things got really bad between us when he admitted that he had had an affair with a secretary at his work. It was horrible, humiliating for me. He was already in a twelve-step program, but I insisted that he leave our house and that we get into family therapy. Therapy made me realize how fragile my marriage had been for a long time and how hard I'd worked to make it stay together. I learned not to feel so responsible for Ted's drinking, or even for the affair. Our older children, Mark and Alison, got really involved in therapy, too—they confronted Ted on his drinking, on his affair. They were angry at me, too, because they felt I had allowed Ted to get away with drinking and running around for too long. Only Chad refused to talk, to get into therapy at all. He didn't get angry, he just wouldn't open up. He watched each of us in those sessions, but he didn't say a word."

I asked Gail, "Was Chad's silence unusual for him?"

She thought for a brief moment and replied, "No, not really. Chad was never much of a talker, so I didn't think that he would unload in therapy, at least not right away. I thought he would benefit by seeing the changes that we were making, like working on our marriage and opening up. I agreed to give the marriage another chance, but on one condition—that we move away, to where I grew up, closer to my family on the Cape, to my support system.

"I had some money put away from an inheritance, and we used it to buy a small place about an hour from the city, very close to my parents. Ted seemed committed to making it work. He commuted on weekends and phoned every day. I really thought we could create a better life, near family. I grew herbs which I sold at a co-op, and I was learning to make cheeses for specialty markets. I could see myself being very successful, someday."

I asked, "How did the family adjust to the move?"

Gail answered, "It was awful for all three kids. Alison had to see a counselor because she was really very sad. She hated school, hated small town life, and saw the move as a selfish solution to save our marriage and family. She had been depressed once before, at the beginning of junior high when we lived in the city, but her friends had helped her through it. This time, though, she didn't have her old friends, and she didn't have it in her to make an effort. The school counselor sent her to a doctor in town, who, after spending only a half-hour with her, prescribed an antidepressant. I wasn't happy with her being on medication. I was even afraid she'd get addicted. You read so many things about drugs."

Gail's fears about antidepressants are very common and rooted in the limited knowledge that most people have about medication. But what had made her the most uneasy was the physician's lack of involvement and very brief interaction with Alison and with them.

"Did the antidepressant help?"

"Yes, I guess so, but she had a lot of side effects. She complained of being light-headed, or else she had headaches a lot. But she stayed on it, mainly because Ted felt strongly that it was important that she feel good emotionally. The doctor agreed.

"Mark had started college in the city already so he didn't need us in the same way, but he and Alison were always close and he was really supportive to her. He came home more often on weekends when she was so depressed. He was home the night Chad killed himself.

"Ninth grade was very tough for Chad. His school counselor thought he might have a learning disability, something that had never been identified before. He had hardly any friends, didn't get involved in anything. He was a real loner. At the end of the school year, Ted and I tried to focus on the positive. We had survived the first year of high school, away from the city and friends, we were together, we were working hard in therapy, the kids were closer to their grandparents. I wanted to reward us, so I blew some of the profits from selling our house in the city on a family trip to California. It was our first family vacation in five years. It seemed to cheer everybody up—at least I thought so. But when we got back, Chad really started to pull away. He would go out at night and not return for hours. When I'd ask where he was, he'd give some excuse. He didn't seem down, like Alison was, but he was . . . I don't know what was so different. I feel horrible saying this, but I didn't know him at all, and I had no idea how to reach him."

The picture of Chad, an awkward, silent boy, was becoming clear. Silence can be interpreted in so many ways. In a family with other problems, like Chad's family, it can mean anger or fear, fear of the future, or fear of breaking down; profound silence, then, is usually a symptom of some painful internal conflict. Even in the most effective therapy, the reality is that you can't force *anyone* to talk, let alone try and come down on a silent, uncommunicative teenage boy. We all struggle with how to interpret a teenager's behavior and solitude. We work very hard with patients like Chad to give them the power, the freedom, the ability to open up, to cry, to scream, and to put into words their inner feelings, if that's what it takes to recover.

Does that mean we should label every silent unresponsive teenager as depressed? Is there a danger in overinterpreting behaviors? Lots of fourteen- and fifteen-year-old boys would be like Chad. I prefer to deal with the silent, nonverbal teen in a therapeutic relationship. Personally, I'd rather be vigilant and suspicious than counsel a family after a suicide. I'd rather look at the silences, the quiet hostility, the anger, as part of the picture of the family problems. There's an old maxim: Often the "bad" or "mad" teenager underneath is the "sad" teen. It may sound simplistic, but in my experience there is some truth to this idea.

I turned to Ted, who was leaning forward in his chair, ready to speak. Gail had talked for nearly twenty minutes. During that time he had loosened his tie. He began: "I think I need to say something now. I didn't want to interrupt Gail before. I know that all these problems come from the fact that our marriage was bad for a long time. I've gone over that ever since the day Chad died. The therapist said I was working long hours to get away from our marital problems. That's only partially true. I'm senior vice president of my company, the only one at that level who's not a part of the CEO's family. It was real tough for me to get that far. You know how I got there? By working my ass off and by being a team player to this day. Nobody in my family appreciates that. My family doesn't understand the effort it takes to be successful. I'm a team player. Mark's a team player, so's Alison. But Gail and Chad—they're happy doing their own thing.

"Okay, I drank too much, I shouldn't have had the affair. I'm even more ashamed about that. When I finally came out and admitted it to Gail, she was hysterical. The affair was over long ago, but she wouldn't even let me stay that night. I spent two months in a hotel. I never wanted to leave the marriage. I agreed to go to family therapy just so we could get back together. What a waste of time! Six months, sometimes twice a week, talk, talk, talk, no answers. The only one who didn't talk was Chad. Gail's right—he just sat there and watched each of us spilling our guts out. Never answered one question that therapist asked. Chad would just look at him, straight in the eyes, and shrug. It bothered me, the fact that he wouldn't talk, and I asked the shrink . . . Uh, sorry, I know you psychiatrists don't like that label; I'm getting carried away."

"I'm not that easily insulted. Go on, Ted, this is important. What did you ask the therapist?"

Ted continued, "I wanted to know if I should be worried that Chad didn't seem to be getting into these sessions, but he didn't like my asking. What did he say? He said that Chad's behavior was a normal consequence of being part of a dysfunctional family." Ted got up and walked around, his hands in his pockets. "Dysfunctional—I'd heard that in twelve-step programs, too. Is the whole world dysfunctional? I mean, with all this confronting that we were doing to each other every week in therapy, you'd think that the therapist would have confronted Chad, maybe asked *him* if he was depressed, or why *he* couldn't talk." He ran his hands through his hair, looking out the window, "I don't think I was asking too much."

Ted's question is a familiar one to me. Many parents have similar questions; they are angry at the failure of professionals to act aggressively. It's not enough to tell grieving parents that teenage depression is often very difficult to recognize.

While I didn't want to appear defensive about another professional, I very much wanted to address Ted's legitimate frustration, his anger that Chad's needs weren't met. "Ted, you're wondering whether Chad's behavior should have been pursued more directly. You want to know why someone couldn't have figured out that Chad had a major problem and was very depressed. Truthfully, it's not always easy to do. Years ago, a colleague told me that working with depressed teenage boys was like a different specialty; he called it veterinary psychiatry. His experience was that with some teens you have to interpret the nuances, the body language, the shrugs. You just can't let go. The more I work with teenage boys, the more I understand and appreciate what he was saying."

I *know* the clues to adolescent depression can be missed. They can be very subtle; in Chad's case, his continued silence and withdrawal were seen as part of adolescence and as reactions to a number of major stressors—the marital problems, Alison's depression, and the move. There were many reasons not to focus on Chad.

Listening to Gail and Ted, I was bothered that Chad had been a spectator at all this display of raw anger and emotion—from Gail and Ted, from Alison and Mark. How was it that he could remain so unemotional? What does it take to unlock a silent teen? Is it persistence or ignoring? My preference is always in persisting, in being tenacious—"the dog with a bone" brand of counseling. I just can't let go. It's not easy, the feedback is not always there, but at some point the silence dissolves. It may erupt in anger or sadness, but the pain comes out, and then it can be treated.

Ted had more to add: "But wait a minute, I'm not done yet, that's the point—we *didn't* leave it. Our family therapist wasn't the only one to treat Chad. We saw that Chad wasn't cooperating; his silence was becoming frustrating for everyone, including the therapist. I never thought he was depressed or wanted to kill himself—nothing like that. But I knew something wasn't right. Chad didn't want to see any more shrinks, but we made him agree to go to one session, with some hotshot Boston psychiatrist, an hour and a half away. The doctor was very reassuring, called me in after the appointment and said that Chad's behavior was a normal response to all the family stress. We gave it our best shot, not once but twice; who are we to argue with doctors? In fact, weeks after Chad died, I called that psychiatrist. It was spur of the moment. I guess I needed to rage at someone, blame someone for not figuring out how crazy Chad was, blame someone besides myself. He told me that Chad had been real friendly, outgoing—I mean, a totally different kid from the one we knew. Chad really did a snow job. It made me think that maybe we should have trusted our instincts."

Instincts! So often parents are afraid to trust their instincts. When I meet with parents and children, particularly in cases where children are very disturbed, I often find that the parents have some awareness that something is very wrong. And yet, when their gut feelings are not validated, what then? In seeking another opinion, Gail and Ted acted more aggressively than many parents. Unfortunately, most parents have neither the access to a variety of professionals nor the insurance to pay for costly assessment or treatment. Psychiatric services for children and adolescents are generally shamefully inadequate and accessible to a disproportionate few.

Teachers, physicians, social workers—we all would like to save every troubled teen, but we can't. The "system" contributes to our failure by providing few and fragmented services for most children and adolescents. The problem is both deeper and broader. It maybe a cliché, but nonetheless, our society values children less than almost any other group. Parents need to rely more on their instincts and, where necessary, to badger the mental health system for answers that work. There are parent advocacy networks in every state.[1] They can provide assistance in guiding parents through the medical and insurance maze.

It was important for me to know more about Chad's family, particularly about any family history of mental illness. Perhaps it was related to his personality problems. I asked, "Was there any history of depression in either of your families?"

Ted nodded, "I don't know about depression, but my dad was an alcoholic, and my mother was always miserable because of her life with him. She may have even had a 'nervous breakdown,' whatever that is. I'm not sure. I don't see my sister anymore. She's had two husbands, and she's been in every type of counseling invented. I can't say that it's helped her. You know, my dad was a loner too, didn't talk much, tinkered with his car and worked in the garden when he wasn't drunk. We never really understood each other. But I never thought I wouldn't understand my own kid." Ted didn't look so tanned anymore. His jacket was on his chair, his silk tie looked crumpled. Ted's obvious pain gripped all of us.

Gail was watching Ted intently. It was clear that she felt enormous sympathy. I expected her to get up and sit next to him, to comfort him, but she resisted. Instead, after glancing at me, and then at her husband again, she continued, "You're asking about family. My parents are very caring. They've always been there for us, especially with money, but they've mostly been pretty tight-lipped. None of us—I have two sisters and three brothers—ever learned to express feelings, negative or positive. Some of us have been in therapy—one of my sisters and two of my brothers—but it's been more to learn how to be open, to deal with conflict more honestly—things like that."

The family history that Gail and Ted shared was sketchy, but some key issues had emerged. There were clear indications of depression, not only in their daughter, Alison, but also in Ted's family. Chad reminded Ted of his own father, a loner, chemically dependent, who dabbled in interests independently and was isolated from the rest of the family. Alison had experienced two bouts of depression, the most recent one requiring a course of medication. Ted, like his father, had a drinking problem, which he attributed to stress; but it is likely that it masked depression. These pieces of the family history suggested lifelong, cross-generational struggles with the pain of depression.

Gail interrupted my mental stocktaking: "Dr. Slaby, do we have time? I have to ask you something else that's bothered me about Chad. You know that there were two other suicides in Chad's school. The first one was a boy who shot himself. Ted and I were both shocked that any kid that young could feel so desperate, so able to take his own life. But Chad, he seemed totally unaffected by it. He was more interested in the type of gun he'd used, where he did it. I couldn't believe that he wasn't shaken up! A couple of months later, a girl killed herself. Her boyfriend had broken up with her and she was afraid she was pregnant. The kids at school had all talked about it for days, and the school counselors held grief sessions. Chad seemed indifferent about her death, too. He seemed more caught up in the TV coverage, the kids being interviewed by the reporters, and all that. I even remember him saying that she had more friends in death than she had ever had when she was alive. It gave me the chills to think that Chad wasn't upset. I decided it had to be because he didn't want us to know how much it bothered him. He had to act macho, tough. I couldn't admit to myself that he had no feelings about these horrible deaths."

"Did Chad say anything about the school counseling, the information he'd received after the suicides?" Gail pondered this question for a few minutes. Ted shrugged, shook his head as if to say no. He had already shut down, exhausted. He shuffled the magazines on the table near the couch, moved the pillow around on the sofa in an attempt to find a more comfortable spot, and finally shut his eyes. Again, Gail answered: "Yes, he talked to me, but mostly in a very matter-of-fact way; he talked about kids crying in the audience and the counselors hugging everyone; he seemed surprised at how badly they felt. In the grief sessions they talked about the finality of suicide. Chad said it was like the credits in a movie. I thought he sounded almost poetic. I never thought for a moment that it had any other meaning. You know, late at night, when I can't sleep, I think about the clues I missed, and I wonder whether Chad knew too much about suicide. Where did he get these ideas? There always seems to be some open dialogue going on at school. Why? I don't remember anyone my age killing themselves when I was a teenager. Are we giving kids too much information? Are we putting ideas into their head?"

Although we were near the end of the session, I couldn't let this line of questioning go for next time. It was a very valid issue. "Gail, it's always been my feeling that there's a fine line between educating teens about preventing suicide and providing them with the knowledge to go out and kill themselves. Most teens aren't so vulnerable that this information would lead to suicide. Personally, when I talk to groups of adolescents, I concentrate more on what the symptoms of depression are and how to link up with professionals. But the truth is that young people are confronted with explicit information about violence all the time. They have to learn how to evaluate the information, how to respond, but not how to model their behavior after it.

"We'll talk more, but not now. You must be exhausted." I glanced at the clock and got up. I had gone over the scheduled first interview by nearly a half-hour. Gail and Ted agreed that at the next meeting Alison and Mark should be included. After they left I closed the office door, ignored the flashing button on the phone, and relaxed. I knew that I had only a few minutes before my secretary would be facing me with a stack of messages and a not-so-gentle reminder about the next patient, who had already been kept waiting far too long. I looked out the window, trying to see beyond the brown brick of the hospital wing in front of me. It was possible, looking at this blue-gray New England sky, to forget that the temperature was only 30 degrees. You might think about skiing and about the days soon getting longer. If you were depressed, though, you might look at that same sky and think about the endless winter, about its bitterness, not unlike the bitterness in your life, in your mind, concluding that neither the cold nor the bleakness in your life would change—not unless you took control, ended it. How do you explain the degree of mental distortion that occurs in depressed teens to a family whose child has made the choice to commit suicide? No matter how compassionate or how straightforward my explanations may be, no matter what comfort families may find in these sessions, it cannot be enough. The pain of parents, siblings, extended family members, and friends after the suicide of a young person is haunting, even when we can provide some answers, some peace of mind, and some comfort.

Two weeks later, all four members of their family were waiting in the narrow, cluttered hallway. Gail extended her hand to me as I arrived. She seemed less tense. Ted had his arm around his older son, Mark, who seemed deep in thought. Their daughter, Alison, looked exactly as her mother had at our first meeting—awkward, tentative. I asked them to make themselves comfortable and explained the purpose of the meetings to Mark and Alison. "It's important for you to understand what motivated Chad. I know this has been very hard for you, but it's critical that you reach some understanding about him and about his suicide. We're not here to blame but to look for those reasons that made life impossible for Chad. When you're ready, please feel free to talk."

Ted was anxious to talk, "I want you to know it was helpful for me to think about those signs you talked about at our last meeting, like Chad's silence. I feel a little better about my own judgment. All this time I felt Chad killed himself to pay me back. I think I'm beginning to accept that Chad didn't suicide to punish us, that he acted on his own. Something else has been bothering me about Chad's death, though. I want to talk about the day he killed himself, about how the police and everyone made us feel like criminals, like we were responsible. It will haunt me for the rest of my life. I feel like I was never able to respond the way I should have."

Glancing around the room, I saw Gail bury her face in her hands and Alison turn away. Only Mark sat rigidly, looking straight ahead. He listened carefully as Ted continued.

"I got a call late that night from Gail. She was sobbing hysterically. I couldn't even make out what she said. It seemed too unbelievable. Chad, dead. How? I thought maybe there was a robbery. I drove home right away. There were police cars everywhere. It was eerie, in the middle of nowhere, just this little house and barn, some fences, and the police and all the lights, ↙ and an ambulance. I was afraid to get out of the car. I just sat in the car shaking. Alison and Mark came running out. 'Chad's dead. He killed himself, hanged himself. It's awful.' They were crying and screaming at the same time. I felt totally paralyzed. I walked into the kitchen—the table set, salads in their bowls at each place. I turned off the oven. I didn't want to go upstairs. I could hear Gail sobbing, screaming at someone, 'Don't touch anything, don't touch him.' I was frozen at the bottom of the stairs."

Sitting next to me, Mark got up, walked out, slamming the door. "I can't stand this. I'll be back." Gail followed him into the hall. Alison watched Ted as he went on, his face flushed.

"The police officer came down with Gail, followed by two ambulance attendants carrying Chad on a stretcher. He was covered up totally. I still cannot bear to remember that sight. The police made an insincere attempt at sympathy while we tried to comfort each other. But soon after, with all of us walking around like crazy people, taking turns running to the bathroom, crying, and phoning family, they sat down and tried to piece it together with us. One officer went upstairs and came down with things from Chad's room. I still don't know all that he took—books, tapes, letters. Nobody gave us a record of what was taken. He showed me Chad's journal and the suicide note, but then he took them away. They sent the suicide note back weeks later with no letter attached, nothing. You can't imagine what it was like to open the envelope and find that. We only got the journal back after Gail called them for days. I don't even know what else they still have. They asked if he'd been abused, or if he was on drugs. They asked horrible questions, whispered to each other a lot, looked at us as if we were criminals.

"It took days before Chad's body was released to the funeral home. Our minister was terrific, even though we hardly ever go to church. He came over right away and spent the night with us. He talked to the newspaper, made all the funeral arrangements, spent a lot of time with the kids. I'll always be grateful to him. The police came over again the next day, wanted to know why we'd been in therapy; all of that had been in the paper. I don't know who told the newspapers we were in therapy. I mean, they made it sound like we were crazy, awful parents.

"The funeral was a circus. Chad was the third student to commit suicide, so people came out of the woodwork. They were everywhere, reporters asking for interviews, asking kids at school who didn't even know him to talk about what Chad was like. His class came to his funeral, but I don't think they came out of any feelings for him. I think it was more because he was the third kid to die and they were terrified. The minister spoke very well, with a lot of feeling for all of us. But how do you do that, get out of your pain? How do you take away those memories—your kid killing himself? How do you ever put the family together again? Stop blaming yourself? Chad shared none of his anger or sadness with us. I always think we didn't matter enough for him *not* to kill himself. Our closest friends were great and so was our family, but most folks were embarrassed to talk to us. Kids avoided our kids. People pretended not to see us in the grocery store, on the street.

"I wanted to sit down, discuss this as a family, but it took a long time before we could even all sit together in the kitchen. I went back to work too soon, only a week later. I couldn't concentrate, and I didn't care about work. I still don't. Gail talked to her therapist and so did Alison, but we couldn't begin to pick up the pieces for a long time."

Gail returned a few minutes before Ted finished his self-questioning. She shook her head, unable to go on from Ted's words. She could only agree, nodding silently. "Maybe this is a good time to show you Chad's journal. We've all read parts of it, but no one's been able to read it all."

Chad's journal was a meticulously kept notebook, with multiple daily entries, the last one being his suicide note. It spoke of a young man who felt like a stranger within his own family. While he acknowledged repeatedly that he knew he was loved, he clearly felt that he didn't fit. He saw himself as too short, puny, and an academic failure. Unlike his siblings, he had few friends, and even they were not "reliable." Some of his entries were desperate, particularly those dealing with the problems in the family.

> Why is everyone going on about Dad's drinking when I'm hurting so much? Don't they see? Alison's depressed. They made sure she got help. How long will it take before I feel different? Will I ever? Every day it's the same thing. Nothing changes.

Chad wrote about a girlfriend. He talked to her every day in class. She seemed to like him, but then, when she was with her friends, she just ignored him. She thought he was just "a friend," she said, just the kid who sat behind her. He was devastated. According to Chad, the shrink he finally went to was a real "dip head," asking all these questions.

> What did he know was in my head? No one knows what's in my head, and nobody ever will. Mom and Dad have their own problems. They'll probably get divorced soon. This family really is screwed up. I hate it. If I die, they'll have one less problem. *me*

Chad had begun to think seriously about suicide after the first student had killed himself six months earlier. He wrote,

> Amazing to blow yourself away and never have to deal with it again. All in two seconds, it's all over. You never have to wonder what's wrong with you anymore. I don't want to hear about my parent's problems anymore. Why should I? Do they look any happier? That's what my life will be like. And my sister, always unhappy all the time. They think I don't notice, but I see it all. The only one who has it together is Mark. I wish I could be like him, he's so cool. Everything he does works, everything I do is a mess, and it never will be better, never will, never will. I love you all. Don't hate me. Just don't forget me, forget me, forget me.

"And in one second, he just did it. Gone and really ruined our family. What a jerk." Those words, spoken so emphatically, so angrily, were from Mark as he returned to the room. "I have something to say," he continued.

"When Chad killed himself, I felt more responsible than anyone else in the family. After I read his journal, I realized how much he looked up to me, how much he wanted to be like me, but we weren't close, ever. The guys he hung around with were the rejects. I'm ashamed of that now, but I was embarrassed by him. He wasn't accepted, cool. If I'd known that he cared about me that much I still don't know if I would have acted any differently. We were all having so many problems dealing with my parents that we really didn't notice Chad's problems. That sounds awful, but how could we know? He never said anything, never did bad things like take drugs or steal or screw around. I went after what I needed—my ticket out of the house was to go to a good college. That's all I cared about the last two years at home. Alison was always a basket case, but she got help real quick. We kind of each did our own thing to survive. You know, last week we watched the video we took when we went to San Francisco. It was supposed to be the trip that brought the family together. Nobody looked very happy, but the weirdest thing was that Chad was in the background in every scene. He was never standing with us, always apart from us. We never noticed it when we were together. Boy, it was a real hard thing to watch."

Alison had been watching Mark while he talked, tears streaming down her face. "Chad once asked me why I was taking medicine when it was giving me such bad stomachaches. I told him stomach trouble is better than being sad all the time. 'There's better ways to end sadness,' he said, 'maybe leave for good, leave this screwed-up family.' I just thought he'd run away. I never thought he'd kill himself." She couldn't even finish talking. Between sobs, she added, "Once, when I was depressed, I thought about killing myself. It scared me so much. That's why I didn't mind taking the medicine."

I could see that Mark and Alison were experiencing tremendous guilt about not recognizing some sign of Chad's depression or his thoughts of suicide. I reassured them, "I know this is hard for you to hear right now, but you couldn't have predicted Chad's actions. He did this entirely on his own. He didn't warn anyone. He had decided in his own mind that suicide was the best and only choice. If he had given you a clue he might have been saved, and he didn't want that."

I wanted to shift the conversation toward their healing: "You've talked about the worst thing that happened—the response from the police, the media, strangers, when Chad killed himself. What helped the most? Alison, can you think of some people who were helpful?"

"I was afraid to walk into school the first day I came back. My homeroom teacher was waiting for me, and she hugged me and let me cry some more before I walked in. She was really supportive, and so was my therapist."

Ted quickly spoke up, "The best thing for me was working with the funeral director. He came and talked to me, wasn't judgmental at all. He knew what to say. I mean, I'd just lost my son. I was in shock. He comforted me and he kept the strangers away from the family. Two weeks later he called and checked up on us and sent us a pamphlet from Compassionate Friends.[2] Mark, didn't you tell me something about someone on your soccer team?"

"That's right. I have a part-time job, coaching a soccer team. One of the sponsors came up to me at the first game and told me to call if I needed anything. His granddaughter had died of cancer and he knew I was hurting. He told me that the next few months would be tough, but somehow I would make it. It meant a lot, especially since I didn't know him well at all. But my friends at school, even in my fraternity, avoided me. I don't think they knew what to say."

Finally, Gail added, "My aunt was great. She really came through, stayed with us for ten days. She kept the house running, bought groceries, fed the animals. You really need someone to run everything because you just can't face day-to-day life. My parents couldn't even speak, let alone function. So they weren't much help."

What was most helpful were the various and many small actions done by professionals, friends, and family in getting through the initial period after Chad's death. Doing what had to be done in a nonjudgmental, supportive, and, most of all, kind way made a difference. If anything was helpful, it was saying things that acknowledged their pain, not minimized it.

It is difficult for friends to find the right words of comfort for any family who has lost a child; when the death is by suicide it is even harder. Not saying anything can be interpreted as rejecting; asking questions may be intrusive and painful. The normal bereavement process, which depends on support, availability, and intimacy with family and friends, cannot take place. Chad's suicide caused an uproar, primarily because his was the third suicide in a short time.

Because of the community's collective concern, Chad's family, after some initial awkwardness, was able to receive some needed support from a number of sources. They continued in several months of intensive therapy with me together; singly; with their minister, Reverend Howe; and at one session, with some friends from the community. They have begun to put the pieces together. While they have accepted the fact that Chad's decision to take his life was his alone, their lives will never be the same.

Mark and Alison are both in college. Alison occasionally has episodes of depression, but she's better at recognizing them and has connected with an excellent psychiatrist. Mark took a year off to work with emotionally disturbed kids and is continuing his studies in psychology. Ted and Gail have made some changes in their lives. Gail sold the farm and they both moved back to the city. She is also in school and is interested in becoming a preschool teacher. Ted left his executive position to work as a lawyer for Legal Aid. In their own way, they are rebuilding their lives. They are also active in a support group, Compassionate Friends, for families who have experienced a child's death.

The group has been an exceptionally helpful experience for them.

■ ■ ■

The experiences described in Chad's case provide some valuable clues for families of children who are suffering from depression. Self-isolation, an inability to share the pain, and denial are all typical of the teen who is severely depressed. Like lots of teen-agers, Chad was able to manipulate professionals into thinking he was just your average teen. It was particularly easy to accept his behaviors when the whole family was going through prob-lems. It could be rationalized that he was upset only because of the family problems; nevertheless, Chad's parents had their doubts. Parents should trust their instincts. If you're uneasy about your child, stick with that feeling. Don't let the teenager convince you otherwise. What you're asking the teenager to do is very difficult. Talking about problems, asking for help, and removing the protective posture of silence are profoundly uncomfortable steps for many teenagers.

Chad's parents were loving and caring. Chad had never overtly indicated the extent of his depression or his frustration. The changes in him were not dramatic, but gradual. He was less happy with his friends, with his looks. His attitude toward the problems in the family was flat and nothing seemed to arouse a significant response. He was not hostile, acting out, or per-forming much worse in school.

Most parents and many professionals would probably have missed the pattern of depression that evolved over time. *What I learned from my work with Chad's family is how subtle and unemotive adolescent depression can be.* Chad's unremitting silence was his loudest cry for help. Nonverbal boys who become suicidally depressed may express their feelings through speeding or other risk-taking behavior. Chad didn't show the risk-taking behav-iors—the ones that would have been a clue to his real feelings. He leapfrogged from being passive and quiet to killing himself. There was no opportunity to respond to his behaviors with the degree of urgency they required. Two previous suicides in the community raised the possibility of suicide in the mind of a vulnerable, depressed boy struggling in a new school, amid family problems. Chad responded with denial, isolation, and suicide.

Three

"THE PUSH/PULL OF OUR RELATIONSHIP"

you're only interested in my weight. I'm miserable skinny and I'm miserable fat why don't you care that I'm miserable? its's gone on too long. it can't get better i'm worn out, i have no more to say to anyone; i have nothing left to paint because everything comes out black. don't be mad at me Derek. you gave me whatever happiness i had no on else could.

I never intended to be a physician who collects suicide notes. It's a ghoulish souvenir of working with families after a child dies from suicide. Usually notes come to me from other physicians, family members, coroner's offices, morticians, clergy; most often I read them weeks or months later, in the context of sessions with families who struggle to understand the tyranny of depression and the depth of a despair that could encompass anyone so completely—especially someone so young. Some notes are long and complicated explanations; others are brief and apologetic. Some answer questions; many raise more issues. So it was for Carly Swinton's family. Her note was attached to her T-shirt when she hurled herself from the top of her dormitory an hour before her scheduled flight home for Christmas vacation. Her bags were neatly packed and her belongings boxed and labeled in her room. Her parents, grandparents, and siblings were waiting at the airport, 1,100 miles away, when the police brought them the terrible news.

My involvement with Carly's family came more than two years after her death. I received a call from a colleague, an internist who was a neighbor of Carly's parents. With their permission, she called to talk about Carly's death, and particularly about the family's overwhelming feelings of guilt and responsibility for her suicide. "In your opinion, Drew, and I know you work with a lot of families, how long should it take for parents, for a family to heal? I mean, they are still just paralyzed. They've had a phenomenal amount of support from friends and from their therapist, but it makes no difference. And these people are savvy—they know what questions to ask, they know where to go for help. Judith and Will—that's their names, Judith and Will Swinton—had problems with Carly for years; they slugged it out in therapy for days and weeks at a time; they stood by her through unbelievable rejection. I mean the *worst*. . . . I think they always knew she might kill herself. But they still can't move on with their lives. I'm concerned that their grieving is taking too long. I don't think it's normal."

How long does "normal" grieving last? How long is "normal" for a widow married six years, sixty years? How does grief differ if the deceased person is old, young, dies suddenly, or suffers a long debilitating illness? And how long is "normal" when a nineteen-year-old daughter decides to end her life? Is the impact of her death greater on the family because she made the choice to die? Or would the bereavement have been as intense had she been killed by a speeding car or by an untreatable illness?

The answers don't come easily. I said to my internist friend, "Truthfully, I don't believe that any family ever really heals completely after the death of a child. Sometimes, if they're lucky, family members can come to terms with it; they might seek comfort in religion, in working with other families, and in reassessing their priorities. With the right support they can reach some inner peace, stop blaming themselves or others, and go about their lives. But even those parents who get to that point come back years later, maybe to relive the last year or to ask different questions. Healing and coping—they're two different things entirely. It sounds like your friends haven't even begun to cope."

She affirmed that the family seemed stuck and continued: "I need some suggestions. There are two older kids, Eric and Lisa, both in college. They've been calling me, asking what to do. I talked to Judith this morning, told her about her kids' concerns, and asked if I could share some information about the family with you, maybe get some advice that could be helpful. I think she'd even be willing to see you; I don't know about Will. Just to give you some idea of the extent of their reaction, Drew, they haven't given away any of Carly's things. Her room is almost like . . . like a shrine—it's really oppressive. But I can't bring myself to tell them that, it sounds so heartless."

As I told her, it's not unusual for parents to have trouble letting go of a child's belongings: "I usually tell parents to save a few things, special mementos, and give the rest away. If kids leave instructions about where they want their things to go— maybe to close friends, or to siblings—it's easy to honor those wishes immediately. But when that doesn't happen, I recommend that clothing and other possessions go to a charity organization where they or their child felt some commitment. It's not helpful to set up a memorial like that in the house. You really can't let go when you have a constant reminder right there. They need to hear that, but gently."

We exchanged some more information about providing support and strength to families in need and closed with some mutual assurances to stay in touch about this particular family.

Weeks later I received a call from Judith Swinton. Her deep voice sounded almost masculine over the phone. She was forceful, direct: "Dr. Slaby, I believe you've spent some time discussing the tragedy in our family with our friend Dr. Ollander. She and our children have persuaded me to call you to arrange an appointment. I think it's only fair to tell you that we have lived Carly's life and her death every day for the last six years. I can't talk about her anymore. If we meet, I only want to talk about how we can put our lives back together. I'd like some assurances that you can respect that."

I was taken aback, not only by her request, but by her manner. She hardly sounded paralyzed; in fact, her agenda was very clear. "Mrs. Swinton, I understand very well that you have been through an unbelievably painful time, but I can't possibly say to you today that if we meet I won't talk about Carly."

"Why not? I have a therapist, and he's been wonderful all through Carly's troubles and her death. I just can't seem to get back into my routine. I need some help with that. I think about Carly's death all the time. And Will, my husband, is unable to help me. I need to get on with my life. That's what I need now. Besides, you never met Carly—you'd only be getting my opinion, my view of her."

"I can only say that in order to go on you may have to go back first. I know it will be hard, especially retelling her history with someone new, but maybe it can be the last time. I can't guarantee that, but we can certainly try."

She was silent for a very long time. "I'll think about it and get back to you. I can't speak for my husband, though."

I heard no more about the Swintons and just assumed that they had chosen not to see me. One morning I noticed their name on the daily patient roster. They were scheduled for a two-hour consultation, the last one of the day. I found the notes about our earlier conversation and put them aside. I usually see the new cases and research consultations at the end of the day, when I feel less encumbered by teaching responsibilities or the phone ringing. At 4:30, when I looked out the door, there was only one person sitting and reading an antique copy of *Newsweek*, one of several vintage magazines that remain after anything more recent has disappeared. She looked up over her reading glasses, "Dr. Slaby? I'm Judith Swinton. My husband will not be joining us today. I assume that won't be a problem." We shook hands and I invited her into the office. Judith Swinton was a tall, striking woman, with considerable presence when she entered a room—broad shoulders, a loping erect walk, short white hair, and clothing that moved in harmony with her angular frame. She glanced around the office, eyeing the worn sofa, the motley assortment of furniture, bookcases, and lamps, and commented, "I guess they're not kidding when they say the university needs money for improvements to their physical plant." I replied, "Believe me, this is the best office on the floor—you should see the others."

I was impressed that she could take this initiative to put me at ease. "I'm glad you came today. Perhaps you don't know about my interest in working with families who have lost a child to suicide. I try to help families gain some insight about their child's depression and suicide. I help them through the next important steps—the ones that are so troubling for you—how to go on and resume a normal life, how to deal with the pain, the guilt, the anger."

"I know why I'm having such trouble coping. I know why I hate to wake up in the morning. It's not just that she killed herself—Carly warned us many times and she tried to kill herself twice before. I feel responsible for her death because she hated me so much and it was because of her hatred for me that she killed herself."

As Judith Swinton spoke, her voice rose dramatically, each word enunciated very deliberately. Her voice and her deep-set blue eyes matched her stiff posture. Her hands were carefully folded in her lap, the late afternoon sun reflected off the rings on her fingers. Adolescence is generally a time when parents and children disagree. Tensions run high, things are said, actions are undertaken in anger and in haste, and afterward everyone is regretful. Parents may not realize that a child is depressed or that he or she is considering suicide. Later they blame themselves for their child's death.

"Mrs. Swinton, when kids are depressed we often have an image of them sleeping all day and moping around, being uninvolved; but another side of depression is anger and hatred. I need to hear more, but perhaps what Carly expressed to you was the anger side of her depression. I'm interpreting your coming to see me as a sign that you'll share information about Carly and your family. Is that fair?"

Judith closed her eyes and leaned her head back. She removed her glasses and clenched them in her lap. "You know until this afternoon I was sure I would cancel this appointment. I relive the last six years of Carly's life every day, like flashbacks, bad dreams that won't go away. I don't know what made me think I could talk about Carly to you. Maybe it's that I have no one else to talk to—nobody can bear to hear it any longer, I can tell. We have great friends, but they don't know how to comfort me anymore. They don't avoid me yet, but they try very hard not to talk about their kids, about their milestones. I remember doing the same thing when Eric was a baby and our dearest friends lost their baby suddenly. I tiptoed around talking about my baby, I didn't share any stories. I knew it was too hard, I knew she had to think, Why me? My husband and I have always had a difficult marriage, and I don't know how we can survive this. I think Will blames me too."

She was silent for a long time. Her eyes were closed and she was working hard to maintain some composure. "Dr. Slaby, Carly did not have depression. She had anorexia. Carly was our youngest child; there's seven years between her and her brother. By the time she came along Will and I were both pretty independent. Will was in the investment business and I had gone back to teaching in a small college. I had less time and patience for Carly and I knew it. She was always such a free spirit, very independent. She was incredibly talented, artistic; Carly was painting before she even spoke in sentences."

"You've talked about her hatred for you. When did that start?"

"Almost from the moment she could talk Carly and I got into power struggles. I used to think it was because she was the youngest and I was too old to deal with a little one again. Her older brother and sister were very easy to raise, but Carly questioned everything. She was always challenging—even when she was little, three or four, she would argue, talk back, and test the rules. The arguments would always end with her telling me or both of us how much she hated us. I remember feeling the same way about my parents, but I never dared say anything even close to that."

"When did she develop her eating disorder?"

"When Carly was about twelve she had her first boyfriend, Derek. We thought she was too young, and we forbid her to go out on dates. She was furious. Soon after that we noticed that she wouldn't eat with us. She found lots of reasons not to eat dinner—headache, stomachache, tired, anything. Sometimes she would only eat apples, or raisins, for days at a time. She took vitamins and drank mineral water, that's all. We ignored it for a long time, thinking it would pass, but then she started to look thin, pale. A school counselor called, suggesting that we get professional help for what she felt was an eating disorder. Carly refused to get help, said there was nothing wrong with her. We tried to be flexible—we said that she wouldn't need to see anyone if she started to eat normally again. For a few weeks it worked, but then she started slipping again, ate poorly, accused me of all kinds of things—reading her journal, checking on her at school, listening in on her phone conversations. She was impossible."

"When did you finally get some help for her?"

"It wasn't her choice to make. One day I found an empty bottle of Tylenol in the bathroom. Carly was asleep in her bed, and I immediately took her to the emergency room to have her stomach pumped. She was groggy but all right. The doctor on call told her very clearly that she—that *we* all needed to get some help and that she would only be released on the condition that an appointment was made. I already had the name of Dr. Weber, who has treated many families we know. In fact, he's chief of child psychiatry at a hospital nearby. You've probably heard about him. He's done a lot of work showing how eating disorders are a family problem."

I was very familiar with Dr. Weber's work. In fact, his videotapes on therapeutic techniques were some of the first to be widely used in psychiatry training programs. His charismatic personality and sometimes unconventional ideas had won him an equal number of fans and detractors.

"Was Carly cooperative in therapy?"

"I wouldn't call it cooperation—more like moving the anger and hatred to the doctor's office. We were in therapy for nearly four years. For the first time we understood how unrealistic our expectations of each other were. We learned how to express feelings, be more honest. Sometimes I think that it destroyed us as a family as much as it helped us. Maybe not saying everything lets you have peace, I don't know anymore. Therapy helped Will to finally leave his job, and now he's a carpenter. He loves it, loves working with wood, making furniture. And Carly, she needed help, desperately. Once she got in, even she knew it—and therapy became the only place she would talk to us. She got closer to her dad in therapy, but she still saw me as the enemy, always. That never changed."

Judith sat up, adjusting her skirt. She twisted her rings nervously on her fingers, checked her watch, and removed it, tossing it beside her on the sofa. She looked at me for a long time. "In therapy, I really learned how much I disliked Carly. When we began, soon after her overdose, Carly, Will, and I went twice, sometimes three times a week. It was tough. Carly directed her anger only at me—how she could never please me, how I had never wanted her to be born. She said that I would rather have had an abortion than have her. Carly brought up fights we'd had when she was eleven or twelve, every painful word I'd said, no matter what she had done to provoke me. Months earlier we had talked about one of her friends who had gained a lot of weight. At the time, I commented to her on how unappealing she looked. It was after that, Carly said, that she decided to get so thin so that I could never be critical of her weight. She believed the reason I didn't want her to have a boyfriend was that I couldn't stand it that anyone else would like her. It was all her interpretation, and in therapy I couldn't defend myself. It brought out all my feelings of resentment toward her. I began to believe that I had failed her, that maybe I really didn't love her."

I was confused. "Are you saying that some of her feelings were true?"

"I've asked myself that every day for the last six years. Why else would she have starved herself? Why else would she kill herself?"

I glanced up at the clock. It was late. I'm constantly amazed at how these difficult sessions don't seem to drag on. They fly by as though only a minute had passed. We needed to have some closure, but not like this. Judith looked up at the clock, "Are we finished for today?"

I responded, "It's late, but before you go there are some things I want to say. You feel very responsible for Carly's suicide, and that's pretty typical. Most parents torture themselves—they think, if I had only been more supportive, if we hadn't had that last fight—there are always lots of questions. 'I drove her to suicide' is something I hear too often. After a suicide, we all struggle with finding out what happened, and until you understand it better you can't go on again. You can't make peace with yourself. But you will do it, you will answer those difficult questions and go on."

Judith opened her purse and handed me Carly's suicide note. It had been crumpled and restored many times. "I can't carry this around anymore. Take it, do whatever you want with it but don't let me see it again. I'll talk to Will . . . about coming next time, I mean. I have a videotape of one of our therapy sessions when Carly was in the hospital. Should I bring it?"

I shook my head. "No, let's wait on that for now. There may be other opportunities, but thanks."

After Judith left, I thought about her two-year struggle with Carly's death and the four years that preceded it. Eating disorders frequently include some element of depression. Starvation and/or bingeing also become the means of expressing anger or feeling in control. In Carly's case she took control to its most destructive climax. I wrote my case notes in the new chart and carefully attached Carly's crumpled note. I shut off the lights. Enough.

Very often, friends ask how I can possibly tolerate interacting with families who have had a child commit suicide. How do I confront this despair in young people who haven't begun to live? Fortunately, I can balance the sad stories with many more that end happily. Working with families struggling with loss and guilt, interviewing teens who have been somehow, miraculously rescued from a suicide attempt—such experiences never become banal, mundane, despite their horrifying repetition in my professional life. The goal is always, always to learn more, to unlock the riddles of depression and to make many copies of the master keys.

At the next appointment, Judith was accompanied by her husband. More than six feet tall and angular in build, Will Swinton was a perfect physical complement to his wife. Sitting in the cramped hallway, in a chair meant for a much smaller person, Will reminded me of how parents look sitting in a kindergarten class for their child's first school play. We shook hands and entered the office. Will's face, deeply lined, taut and weathered, seemed etched in granite. He sat on the edge of the sofa, at the angle furthest from me. I could guess that his response to me would be negative before we even began to speak.

I began: "I'm glad you came today, Mr. Swinton. I have a sense that coming here was very difficult for you. Your wife has shared some background with me already. It would be helpful for me to also hear what you have to say."

Will hesitated and then spoke frankly: "Dr. Slaby, look . . . I appreciate what you're trying to do here. It's true, we haven't been able to put Carly's death in the past. But we have a therapist already, and I feel disloyal coming to see you. It's not that he hasn't helped, he's been there for us all the time. Truthfully, I didn't want to get mixed up with anyone new. I'm here for Judith, she's the one who can't seem to let go. I did that a long time ago."

I assured him that this wasn't a therapy competition. "I'm pleased that you have had so much support and excellent help. I don't see myself replacing your therapist, but sometimes families need a fresh perspective, some new ideas. Continue to see your therapist, but maybe you can see these meetings as a process which can help you understand Carly's suicide and your response to it."

Will seemed to digest this, and relaxed noticeably. The lines in his face seemed to soften. He sat further back in the sofa, turning toward Judith. "I really don't know what to say. I've been through this so many times. Judith tortures herself because she knows she was strict with Carly, much more than with the other two. She knows that if she'd eased up a little, Carly wouldn't have had to fight her so much, she wouldn't have starved herself."

Judith had heard this before. Her response was immediate, "You always sound like this was all my fault. You forget that Carly would always run to you when she didn't like the rules. It was you who wanted me to ease up when she started to diet. Besides, everything got worse when you quit your job. She couldn't understand that you did it for yourself, not because of her. She wouldn't hear that you wanted to spend more time at home, with her, with me. She even blamed me for your quitting. You didn't deny that either. And as I recall, you didn't try and stop her from leaving for college even though she looked like a skeleton."

Will stood up suddenly, and for a moment I thought he would slap Judith. I looked at him evenly. Will raised his hands to me as though to say, "Stop, it's okay." He responded, "Are you happy now, Judith? You're playing your victim role again for the doctor. We've rehashed this so many times, I'm sick of it. I didn't stop her because I knew how desperate she was to leave you. I knew she couldn't heal in our house, not with you fighting with her over every little thing."

Judith got up and faced Will squarely, "Well, she healed just fine, didn't she?" He started to respond—his curse at Judith was on his lips—but he stopped short, took out his wallet, and removed a picture, extending it to me wordlessly. It was a high school graduation picture of a beautiful red-haired girl, with her mortar board perched at a rakish angle, the tassel covering part of her face. Add age lines and thirty years, and you saw Will's face. I turned it over and read the inscription: "to my comfort and spirit, from your loving thorn."

The recriminations, ugly and hurtful, that may lie dormant in a marriage, festering, bubbling beneath the surface, are quick to rise in a crisis. This was clearly old territory for the Swintons, and it explained why Judith could not move on, why Will, prob-

ably, was also not able to deal with their tragedy. I didn't want
this session to deteriorate into one more battle. There were more
important issues. I interrupted them.

"It's totally understandable that you lash out at each other.
But it seems to me that you're blaming and judgmental because
each of you has only a partial sense of what drove Carly to suicide. And until you have some deeper understanding, it will be
impossible for you to resolve your grief."

Will and Judith sat down again. They were embarrassed.
Their unexpected and passionate expression of raw anger was
not something they would have wished me to witness in our
first joint session.

Even if they were skeptical of what I had to say, they were
chastened. I continued, "Above all else, eating disorders are a
way of exercising control. Just now, each of you was trying to
exercise some control by blaming the other. Carly may have
been fighting for control with her mother all the time. With each
issue, the stakes got higher, until finally she took control of her
inner pain and stopped it forever through her suicide."

Control is always a tough call. When is it too much, or when
does a lack of control create chaos in a teenager's life?

"Judith, you saw Carly struggling, and by intervening in her
best interests, by imposing limits, by insisting that she maintain
a reasonable diet, you were confronting her on each issue.
Because her dad was more ambivalent and picked his battles,
Carly could blame you. By escalating the issues she was able to
draw you into battle each time."

Judith was listening, tears streaming down her face. She dis-
solved into loud anguished sobs, her whole body shaking. Will
made no attempt to comfort her. He sat rigidly, biting his lower
lip. Judith regained her breath, and began to speak, "What do I
do now? How can I ever live with myself? I always knew I
should stop, not say another word. But she was wasting away
every day, she was throwing away her life. I would have been a
worse mother if I'd let it all go by, if I'd watched her waste away
. . . wouldn't I?" She started to cry again.

"Judith, you responded as most loving parents would. You

want to protect your children, you don't want them to stumble and fall. It's not unreasonable to limit dating at an early age, and of course you wanted to stop the starving. But Carly was really saying, 'Let me live my own life. I'm not you, and I've got to find my own place.' "

Will was staring at Carly's picture in his hand. "You know, we went through a lot of this—all of this—in therapy with Carly. I remember, she said, 'It's my life, mine, not yours.' So we would strike a deal, we even made contracts. Carly could stay out late one night in the weekend, not two, and then we wouldn't bug her. Or she could talk to Derek, her boyfriend, every night on the phone for a half-hour, not an hour. If she ate only part of her supper, we wouldn't make an issue of it. Judith tried to let go, sometimes she just left the room rather than continue. I was just better at it than she. Besides, Carly didn't force the issue with me all the time. She did with Judith. Dr. Weber said it's more of a mother-daughter thing, the battles."

Judith winced. Her face was blotchy with hives, her hair was disheveled and wet from perspiration. "Are we almost through?" she asked. "I'd like to go home."

Will took her hand and started to get up. I thought about how stressful it is to re-create the past, to fill in the blanks, to probe the worst nightmares about a child who couldn't be reached. "Before our next meeting, I'd like you to think about the fact that control was only one part of Carly's need. At times, girls with eating disorders tend to be very depressed. And if we don't isolate and treat the depression, we're only treating a part of the problem."

As Will and Judith left the office, I hoped they could somehow integrate the reality of depression more completely into their understanding of Carly's illness and her decision to kill herself.

As I reviewed my notes and looked for the most helpful messages to convey next time, I recognized the qualities that tied it all together: the intensity of Carly's feelings and her struggle over her dependency needs, both so typical of interactions with teens who are profoundly depressed. When adolescents become depressed, they believe they have even lost control over their own feelings. They'll go to a rock concert or a movie thinking they'll feel better, but the boost doesn't last more than the evening. All the intense feelings return the next morning, when they may feel even more sad and out of control. Nothing seems to work. Consequently, they rely on others more to raise their spirits, because they can't count on themselves.

Depression and dependency personality traits usually appear together in a young person, like a matched set. Mother-daughter dependency is usually intense in girls with depression, and still higher in girls with eating disorders. Sometimes, a dependent personality disorder emerges without any evidence of depression. Frustration for both mother and daughter increases as the teen fights her dependency needs and reliance on others by challenging, arguing, and using the anorexia or bulimia as a weapon against her closest authority figure, usually her mother. This is not real independence. Mother may try and stop the abnormal behaviors out of concern and fear. She may impose controls, insist on professional help, argue; for her efforts she is rewarded not with compliance but with constant escalating conflict with the child. The child feels a continued pressure to intensify, to accelerate the divisive problem behaviors. Ultimately, both mother and daughter label mother as the source of the problem.

Indeed, Judith's own intense dependency needs as a parent motivated her to try very hard to force some kind of relationship with Carly, regardless of the quality of their interactions. Two weeks later, when I saw her again, Judith had not let go of her feelings of responsibility. By accepting Carly's explanations, especially her insistence that her mother was responsible for her unhappiness, Judith blocked any path to resolution. Memories of the conflicts that preceded Carly's suicide only stoked the flames of Judith's guilt.

It is always difficult to heal after the death of a child. A child's death is a devastating assault on nature, on the natural order of life. Neither Judith nor Will fully understood the complexity common in eating disorders, the interaction of depression, dependence, and the struggle for autonomy and control.

I met with the Swintons twice more in the next three months. At each of our meetings, we reviewed these issues. They gradually came to understand the forces that drove Carly so mercilessly and to accept their own unwitting, unintentional contribution to maintaining Carly's anger and tension.

At our final meeting, they mentioned that they had attended a meeting of Survivors of Suicide and had found it very helpful. Their therapist had encouraged them to attend a meeting shortly after Carly's death, but they had been unable then to muster the courage to attend. They called me six months later to tell me that they had donated Carly's clothing, bedroom furniture, and books to a shelter for abused women. They distributed her artwork and pottery to friends and family, saving only a few special paintings for themselves.

It seemed that Judith and Will were finally able to start healing and moving beyond the tragic pain of Carly's suicide.

∎ ∎ ∎

Carly's case reminded me of the intimate link between eating disorders and suicide. Physicians are very aware of the high mortality rate among people with anorexia nervosa and bulimia nervosa.[1] It is commonly thought that the high death rate results from starvation and other metabolic irregularities. This assumption is only partially correct. Death from suicide is much more common than deaths from the eating disorder itself. Teens with eating disorders frequently are self-destructive and have recurring thoughts of suicide. Some clinicians even consider the eating disorder symptoms as chronic, progressive, insidious acts of self-destruction. Extreme starvation can be viewed as a chronic suicidal pattern, and must be treated as a life-threatening pattern.

Carly and her mother were in a hostile and conflictual relationship based on their struggle around dependency on each other. Typically, when battles around children's autonomy occur, parents are unable to distance themselves from their children's decision making. All too often, parents are pained by their offspring's independent decisions, which result in such apparently dire consequences. Can parents sit on the sidelines watching their children make mistakes? If the mistakes are minor ones, the psychological equivalent of skinned knees, parents can sit, watch, and appreciate the lessons being learned by their children. The potential for bigger, more devastating mistakes motivates parents to provide more advice and direction. Life-threatening mistakes should lead to physical intervention by the parents.

Carly's parents taught me that intense anger surrounding the conflicts before the suicide only impedes the resolution of bereavement. Parents who have fought with their child up to the moment of suicide not only feel guilty, but also have trouble letting go of the conflict and accepting the finality of the suicide. How can parents accept the death and the act of suicide? A positive relationship, bound by mutual respect and not predicated on conflict, allows survivors to accept the finality of the suicide and to let go of their self-blame. Will's relationship with Carly was less conflicted than Judith's and his laid-back parental style allowed Carly to experience more autonomy. He was better able to establish closure on her death and end his bereavement. Judith, on the other hand, had not let go of the conflicts she experienced with Carly. Until she understood the struggle for independence that she unwittingly engaged in with Carly, the pain of her bereavement remained unabated. In this case, the different parental styles that the parents brought into the marriage created different rates of resolution and completion of the mourning process. Resolution comes with healing, and healing with putting to rest and letting go of the struggles from the past.

Four

ACCEPTANCE

John Joseph Pacelli was seventeen years old to the day when he shot himself to death.

Before becoming an assistant to a corporate president two years earlier, Mary Pacelli, John's mother, had worked as an executive secretary at my hospital for ten years. Consequently, she was very familiar with my work with families of children who have committed suicide. She called and met with me several months after John's death.

Tiny, not even five feet tall, Mary had doll-like features. She looked ten years younger than her thirty-eight years. Although Mary and I had a long-standing and comfortable relationship, she found it very difficult to speak about the significant issues that triggered her son's suicide. As long as I was talking about John's schoolwork or his attachment to her, she was comfortable. Beyond that, information had to be drawn out ever so slowly, in tidbits. Over the months I met with her, she became even more diffident and tense than a new referral who must sit down and share his or her history for the first time.

When we met initially, though, she clasped my hands tightly, comforted at the prospect of seeing an old friend. She began sobbing as soon as we sat down together: "I know it's only a few months since he died, but I can barely talk to anyone about

John's suicide. John was my whole life, and he knew it. How could he do this? We were so close. I never had a moment's worry from him, and then this. If I'd had any warning, but nothing, nothing at all." She convulsed in tears, her tiny frame shaking. "I used to see those kids coming into your office. I'd see those parents, and I'd go home and thank God for my wonderful son, even though I was alone, and even though Paul never sent a penny, never even called to find out about his son. I was still so grateful. And here I am, just like all those others, no different."

"These are very painful meetings, I know, but you're here now, and I want to help you; we can walk through this together." I brought in some tea, and Mary gratefully sipped it, slipping a pill onto her tongue.

"A sedative," she explained hesitantly, between sips. "I've been taking them so that I can sleep at night and get up in the morning. I don't even know where to begin. I guess you want me to describe John." She was listing his qualities mentally as she spoke. "He was very . . . sensitive . . . artistic, a perfectionist, always an A student all through school, except for gym," she added with an approving smile. "But very nervous—very, always. Even when he was younger, in elementary school, he would cry before going to school, and when he came home, he was always saying the teacher didn't like him, or he wasn't invited to a birthday party. He was always the last one picked for sports, and then the kids would call him sissy, wimp, mama's boy." She took a deep breath. "I guess he was a mama's boy in a way; he had to be. He was only five when Paul walked out, and other than my brother and my father, there were no men in his life. Not too many in mine, either. I didn't want anyone to interfere in our lives while he was growing up."

The perfectionism John aspired to is a common thread among suicidal adolescents. They must be "all" or they are nothing. This demanding, uncompromising attitude becomes a setup for their own perceived failure, depression, and sense of hopelessness. Hopelessness, in turn, can lead to suicidal thoughts, and suicidal thoughts may yield to suicide attempts.

I learned that John was a highly gifted artist. He had taken art classes at school and at art galleries since he was a young boy. Mary said that even when money was very tight she or her parents made sure that he had art classes. But as he grew up, John shared fewer of his drawings and paintings with his mother. It was only after his death, when she found some of his work stored under his bed, that she saw the vividly painted expressions of rage and sadness in his work. The people in his pictures were all in their death throes; the landscapes were devastated wastelands, like the remains of a nuclear disaster. They graphically attested to the pain he must have been feeling. In retrospect, these were clues to his state of mind. I asked Mary if she found the art disturbing or merely artistically expressive.

"They were under his bed, that's where I found them. At first, I was stunned. Most of them were frightening. I honestly don't know what I would have done if I'd seen them when John was alive. But I think they have more meaning to me now than when he drew them. There was one picture of a young man locked up in a padded cell. That one I'd seen before. John had it hanging in school. It even won an award in a school competition. When I thought about that picture more, I recognized it. It was like a game we played in Dungeons and Dragons. John and I were into that a lot, and into mythology. Once I figured that out, and looked at the pictures again, I wasn't as upset by them."

"Was there anything else you found that surprised you—letters, books, anything?"

She hesitated for a moment, deliberating whether she should say anything: "I know I have to tell you this. It would have come out at some time. I did find a sex film. But you must believe me; it wasn't like John at all, I know it. I found it under his desk, and I just threw it out. Later I got it out of the garbage because I wanted to see it, see if there was anything violent in it. And for a while he got a sleazy magazine, *Heavy Metal*. It wasn't like a sex book, but it's an adult comic book, the type of thing with a lot of naked women in it, and naked men too. But my brother, he used to have magazines like *Hustler* and *Playboy*. He used to hide them under his mattress. That's not abnormal, is it, for guys?"

"No, it's pretty typical for boys to seek out erotic magazines and films. What was in the movie?"

Mary rolled her eyes. "Oh God, this is really . . . it was a movie with a lot of naked men—not boys, *men*—and there were men and women beating them. Oh please, I hate even telling you about this. I only got through part of it because it was so vulgar. It made me sick. It makes John seem so dirty, and he wasn't, I tell you, he wasn't. He's dead, isn't that enough?"

I wondered if she knew of any sexual concerns, any sexual problems John may have had. She objected to the question. "Sex problems? No, of course not. I would never ask a boy like John about his sex life. I mean, of course, he didn't have one. He had girlfriends in high school, but he wasn't into partying, drugs, drinking, none of that."

Recurrently, in cases of sudden, unexplained suicides of sensitive, artistic young men, I have learned that they had lived with the conviction, real or otherwise, that they were homosexual. Consumed with shame, terrified of the censure of their family and friends if they were suspected, they struggled for months, sometimes years, until something triggered a severe depressive episode.

Most adults who openly acknowledge their homosexuality do so only after wrenching personal struggle; openly acknowledging homosexuality in adolescence is far more complex. At this age teens grapple with defining their sexuality; the knowledge of a gay teen among them is incredibly threatening and raises self-doubts, fears, and of course, in today's world, hysteria about AIDS. Questions like: "Will he come on to me?" "If he is attracted to me, what does that say about me? Does that mean I come across as gay?" are typical.

I asked Mary if she thought John might have doubted his heterosexuality. Mary emphatically rejected this possibility. "No way! He was no fairy. Are you telling me that every artist is a fairy? John knew how perverted that life is." I hadn't expected Mary's openly intolerant attitude. Her fears about John were obviously there. As I learned more about John, and once Mary became more comfortable, I wondered if it would be possible to suggest that her obvious bias would have precluded any meaningful discussion about sexuality.

When she read the surprise on my face, she hastened to add, "Look, I'm not apologizing for what I feel. Why would any mother want her child to be gay? John wanted to be a doctor, not an artist. Art was only his hobby. I thought he'd be an architect and use his art that way, but he wanted to be a doctor so he would never have to worry about money. I remember once saying to him, 'John, you should go into pediatrics. It's so great to see kids get better.' I was thinking about my years at the hospital. I would see the children come in, and they would be in bad shape; then after a few weeks, or months, you could see they were much better. And he looked at me very seriously and said, 'No, I couldn't do that. If anything ever happened to a kid I was looking after, I would kill myself.'

"But then, another time, he said he would kill himself if he didn't get into medical school, but I didn't pay any attention to it. Kids say things. We all do, you know, like saying you'll kill yourself if this or that doesn't happen. When I lie awake at night thinking of him, I remember how he was always saying things like that. He had to have things a certain way, his way. Otherwise he was afraid of life, of what would happen to him. My God, when I hear myself say that out loud . . . isn't that an awful thing to think about your own boy?"

"No, not especially. It tells us that you accepted him for who he was, with all his anxieties. What about friends? Did John have many friends?"

"I guess you figured out by now that John never really fit in with the 'in' crowd at school. His friends were the 'nerds,' a lot like him. They were all on the math team and the science team at school; they stuck together after school too. They'd come over to play chess, or do weird things with the computer, play Dungeons and Dragons. They were okay kids."

For some teens, and in some schools, avoiding drugs and drinking, not excelling in sports, and not being part of a crowd

guarantees social isolation and labels them as weird. Social con-
tacts become an ongoing source of stress and anxiety. Some
adolescents become involved in drugs and sex, even crime and
violence, in order to be accepted and to be part of a social group
at school and/or in the community. John, however, had no difficulty rejecting those pastimes; he had his own goals.

Over the next six months, despite Mary's increasing reluctance to provide information, I developed a profile of John—a
young man consumed with exceptional drive and talent, and
at the same time, someone who placed extraordinary demands
on himself.

Mary marveled at his accomplishments: "He never had any
trouble finding jobs; sometimes he held two or three at once—
tutoring, working as a stock boy, anything. He even invested in
copper and antiques. How many kids do you know who buy
antiques? He had nearly eight thousand dollars in the bank and
he was accepted into every college he applied to. But money
was a problem for the better schools—the Ivy Leagues—where
he wanted to go. Harvard would have been his first choice. He
didn't want a state school and he couldn't get enough tuition
help for Harvard. That's why he was so money hungry in high
school."

As I thought about the antiques and the coins, I wondered
whether John had ever gone on buying sprees or had in any
other way demonstrated manic behavior. I explained the concept to Mary and asked her.

"No, never, just the opposite! He thought about anything he
bought for days. He'd buy something, return it the next day,
and then go back a week later to buy it again. And then it would
start over. It used to drive me nuts. He would go to these old,
dirty stores, looking for a bargain, and then he'd argue over the
price. My mother used to say shopping with him was like being
back in the old country, in Portugal."

John's frugality and concern about money were not characteristic behavior of bipolar illness (manic depression), in which
spending sprees are common. To John, money might well have
represented the ultimate tool to control his future security.

It seemed to me that John's behavior could be understood as falling within a pattern of behavior characteristic of an obsessive personality disorder. I was uncertain whether Mary was able to see this, whether she could accept her son as less than perfect.

One day she began our meeting, "A while ago you asked me what answers I was hoping to find in our meetings. I think about that every time I come here. The hard part for me is that I know I'm looking for answers, but I'm afraid to hear them. Do you know what I mean? John must have had problems. Is there something that a person has . . . that you can notice? Oh, God, I'm not making any sense, am I? Well, I guess I didn't see it. Maybe all I would let myself see were John's talents. I must have ignored his pain."

I responded, gently, "Your worst fear is that the answers you may find will be too horrifying. But let's see where we can go with this. Tell me more about the last year."

"He was so scared about college. He really worried about it all last year, worried about not making it, about not having friends, just like when he was little. It was just the same."

Many seniors feel a sense of panic on the threshold of leaving the familiar and beginning a new life away from family and friends. They have doubts about their ability to succeed, to make new friends. John's fears weren't that unusual. But if those fears alone were enough to propel him into depression and suicide, they were symptomatic of far more serious problems.

I asked Mary, "Do you think his fear of going to college had anything to do with feeling responsible for you?"

"I never ever made him feel guilty about leaving, if that's what you mean. I encouraged him, I was totally clear that he needed to leave me. We talked about it a lot. No, never! It was more about beginning a new life. Yes, we were very close, he was my only partner. In that way, he was an adult. But he had to be independent from the time he was seven. I worked full-time then, you remember, when I was at the hospital, and he went to a baby-sitter right from school. Don't you remember the times I had to go and get him and bring him to work when the sitter was sick? It isn't easy, believe me. And I only had one kid, and God, now he's gone."

Mary and John's father, Paul, had been high school sweethearts when they married. Mary was four months pregnant. The marriage rapidly broke down and they finally divorced when John was five, after two years of separation and bitter acrimony. Paul had quickly realized that he had married too young and resented the responsibilities and pressures of marriage and especially of a child. Chronically without work, he turned to alcohol and verbal abuse to cope with his own limitations. Mary, a devout Catholic from a traditional, working-class, immigrant Portuguese family, did everything to keep the marriage together, even as Paul's behavior became more erratic. But once he left, Mary threw herself into the task of being both mother and father.

Wanting to fill out the picture, I asked, "Mary, we've talked about the problems in the marriage, but what was Paul like, before the problems began?"

"We were both such babies. Sometimes I can't remember that time before, when we were in high school. Maybe John was like his father in some ways. I don't know anymore. Paul was afraid of a lot of things too. Until he met me, he didn't have girlfriends; he was too shy. I remember he was always terrified when teachers called on him in class. Until I got pregnant, he was good to me, but when my parents insisted that we get married, he freaked out. Even though we'd been together a long time, he wanted things to stay the way they were. It was a real mistake to get married. Paul saw John from time to time, until he got to junior high, and then it stopped when he got remarried. My mother tells me that Paul just left his second wife. You know, he never even came to the funeral. He said he would when our priest called him, but he never showed up. What a bastard!"

"How did John do after the divorce?"

"I don't know if the divorce made a difference to John. Paul hadn't been there for him for so long that he barely knew him. When John was about seven or eight, his teacher recommended that he get some help because he seemed so nervous, so different in class. He'd be sad for the whole morning after I would drop him off. He wouldn't play much with the other kids. Like me, maybe he was afraid he'd be dumped, too. He did see the school psychologist for almost six months—that way I didn't have to pay. But nothing came of it."

"The psychologist said everything was all right?"

"Not exactly . . . She said John wouldn't share much, which I had already told her would happen even before he walked in there. In her opinion," Mary said with some sarcasm, "what he really needed was a male role model." But that's the line they give all single mothers. That, and don't be so overprotective.

"Were you able to do that? With your dad, or your brother?"

"My dad is old-country Portuguese. He was never the type to play ball, do American guy things. He came home from his job—he was in construction—and he was dead tired. He wanted his supper, his newspaper and his TV, so he could fall asleep. He worked five years more than he should have, just so he could help me if I needed it. My brother tried for a while to do things with John, but he was young, more interested in girls and fast cars, not a little nephew. I tried 'Big Brothers,' but I could never get John hooked up with someone for long. It seemed that as soon as John got attached to someone for a few months, they'd quit because it took too much time. It was so frustrating, and in the end, it was worse because he kept feeling rejected. I stopped trying after a while. It wasn't worth it."

What constitutes a family unit in today's society is dramatically different from what it once was. And the change has come relatively quickly, primarily in the last fifteen years. Not only is the nuclear family in the minority, but it also no longer represents the only positive model. I try hard to promote the philosophy that the critical components in a family are stability and loving adult figure(s) to provide strength and emotional growth for all children in the household. Emotionally whole children thrive in single-parent families, blended families, interracial families, gay and lesbian families. Unfortunately, our social, educational, and mental health services have not adapted to these changes as quickly. And for single parents, the burden is especially heavy, even more so when the parent and child are of the opposite sex. We may have progressed in the choices available to men and women, but generally our responses to these radical shifts in family life remain antiquated.

After several meetings with Mary, I had a better idea of some of the factors that had intersected on John's path to tragedy—a sensitive, artistic, confused young man, and a loving, supportive, somewhat dependent mother, trying to find the optimal place in each other's lives. Much of John's behavior was similar to that of other boys his age. Clearly, he was insecure, anxious, socially awkward, reclusive, and driven. Taken individually, these characteristics did not constitute unusually alarming signs of depression or suicidal behavior. It was only because I have seen and talked to so many depressed young men with this same profile that I cautiously prepared my questions for our next meeting.

I asked Mary to help me broaden my understanding of John's temperament.

She responded: "I've told you all this before. He was so unrealistic. He would say something like, 'When I'm a doctor, I don't want to treat anyone who might die, like someone with cancer.' But to my mind, he was just a kid. What did he know? He'd learn about dying in the first week of medical school. Where are you going with all this?"

Mary was becoming more frustrated with our meetings. She wasn't sure if she wanted to continue: "I don't understand why it happened, but most of all, I knew if I came here like all those other parents, it must mean it was really true. But why can't you tell me why he did it? All these questions . . . it's hard enough to admit it's really happened. He's dead. I can't pretend he's away at college. He's gone—forever." Mary's eyes filled with tears.

"Are you ashamed that he committed suicide?"

"I don't think I'm ashamed, but I'm uncomfortable, even with friends, and especially with my family. I avoid people. I think that sometimes they look at me like they know some awful secret about me. Even at work I don't go to the cafeteria for lunch; I eat at my desk. I hate when people come up to me and say, 'I'm sorry about your son. What happened?' If I tell them how he died, they don't know what to say, and if they do know, they look at me with these pitiful looks. I hate it! I don't want them to say, 'I know what you're going through.' It's something I hope they'll never know."

Usually the funeral service is a very important beginning in the process of at least acknowledging the reality of the child's death. But Mary had only a fragmentary memory of John's funeral: "I look back and I can't even remember the wake. I don't know what John looked like there in the casket. I don't know who picked out his clothes, or what he wore. All I remember is the priest, and my mother screaming when they put him in the ground. I can't even believe it now, but I went right into John's room a week later and sorted things out. I was like ice. That's when I found the pictures under his bed. I gave away books, tapes, and all his art supplies. Only his clothes—I couldn't touch his clothes. He used to line them up in his closet by color. I just couldn't break them up, but I will, I will."

John's compulsive behavior was sometimes the target of derision from Mary's friends. When her bridge group came over, he would sweep up any crumbs while they were still eating and empty the ashtrays as soon as someone put out a cigarette. Her friends used to joke that he should forget medical school and run a cleaning service instead.

But John had always been his own person, and Mary was able to rationalize his eccentricities. She was never put off by his character. It was only much later that she revealed that in his last few days of life his habits totally changed.

"He went on a winter camping trip, and after that he was changed. I don't know why. He didn't get along with someone on the trip. I don't really know the truth. He came back a day early—said he wasn't feeling well. It seemed logical. For a couple of days he wasn't eating. He stayed in his bathrobe all day, didn't shave, shower, or leave the house. He did go to school one morning, but he came home early, after some problem at school. He wouldn't talk about it. He didn't show up for work two days in a row at a new job, and didn't bother to call, so he was fired."

"It sounds so unlike him to be that irresponsible. Can you remember anything else, something different, that happened?"

Mary was evasive, then snappish: "Don't you think I want to know the same thing? I told you, he went camping with three other boys the weekend before he died. That's it. That's all I know!"

"Who were the boys he went with? Did you know them?"

By now, Mary seemed very absorbed in her own thoughts. We took a break so she could have some time alone. When I came back, she seemed more composed.

"After John died, maybe a week later, I called one of the boys who went on the trip. He was very odd on the phone, said he was too busy to meet with me. He would only say that John left early because he wasn't feeling well. I don't know why you're making so much of this trip. Maybe these guys were drinking or doing other things he didn't like. He couldn't tell me, that's all." She stood up and looked at her watch. "I really must go . . . I'm tired. I have an appointment. I have to think some more." Mary, agitated and defensive, was uncomfortable with being totally direct with me. She was holding back, unable to speak; this was likely at the root of why she had originally come for help.

Mary called the next day to apologize for her abruptness, saying she'd been having trouble sleeping for weeks. I reassured her; I know how hard these meetings are.

She continued: "You know, for the first time since he died, I've been dreaming about John. My dreams wake me up at night. I never had these dreams before. Why now? Usually I don't remember my dreams. Why, all of a sudden, are they so clear? Why?"

"Maybe these dreams are emerging because you've begun to accept the loss."

She was relieved: "I feel better then. I was afraid I was slipping. I thought I was going backward instead of forward."

Dreams help us to integrate different aspects of our life, in some cases our past and our present. Sometimes dreams may be a way of imagining socially unacceptable or aggressive feelings. For Mary, her sudden painful loss couldn't be openly acknowledged or accepted. She had to replay all the reasons she could imagine for John's unhappiness. In our earlier sessions we had talked about her husband and about John's fears about leaving. She had woven these pieces into her dreams, into her heavy sadness at John's death. At our next meeting, Mary seemed more open to working on some issues.

I asked, "Was John close to anyone else in the family besides you?"

Mary nodded, "My mother. He played into my mother's need to compete with me. She adored him. She spoke to him maybe fifteen minutes before he shot himself." Mary could not hide her bitterness toward her mother. "She hasn't let me forget it either."

"Has anyone in your family been diagnosed with depression?"

"What's the matter? No easy questions today? Yes, me. Many years ago, when I was eighteen and very mixed up, I was very depressed, but John never knew. I didn't tell him. I don't see it that way but I guess you'd say I made a suicide attempt. I swallowed twenty aspirins. Any time I've thought about it since, I'm so ashamed. I don't know what I was thinking, except I wanted to sleep for a long time. I hated being eighteen and living in my mother's house. I had to get out of this horrible rut. I was sleeping with Paul, terrified I was pregnant. It was a mess. It was my wake-up call. You know, do something drastic! I even called 911 as soon as I swallowed those aspirins. I got out of the hospital the next day, and three months later, I got a job and an apartment away from my mother. I went on with my life."

The best and most lasting insight is that gained through self-discovery. But insight can be illusory. Sometimes only specific, tough questions work. When we're not confrontational, it becomes easier to avoid the truth. So often in our interviews, parents will say, "Until now I didn't know anyone who has ever attempted suicide, and definitely, I never knew anyone who died by suicide." In truth, they often know someone who killed himself or herself. They may even be related, but they never wanted to know the truth. Such massive denial allows them to continue a pretense, remain insulated, not vulnerable. Mary chose to remember her overdose as trivial; indeed, only reluctantly did she call it a suicide attempt.

"At that moment, when you took those pills, do you remember at all what you thought would happen?"

"You don't need to ask me the next question. I'm not an idiot. I know what you're thinking. Of course, I've thought about it more since John killed himself. When I took those pills, I wasn't thinking of dying, only about getting back at my mother. I told you I called for help right away. You can bet that my mother reminded me about that night more than once after John killed himself."

Mary's experience was the textbook young person's suicide attempt, the "risk and rescue" phenomenon. She was probably reacting to a buildup of anxiety and frustration. She had some innate capacity to get help, and she truly didn't want to die.

"Had you felt depressed for a while when you took those pills?"

"I was always very weak—emotionally, I mean. Is that the same as depression?" She didn't wait for an answer. "I let my mother dominate me, force me to get married. That's probably why, in the first couple of years of our marriage, things were so bad with Paul and me. There was nobody I could go to for help; it was different then. I was ashamed, pregnant, trapped. This is going back almost twenty years."

"Did you ever think John felt trapped?"

Mary shook her head: "What you're really asking is should I have thought he might do what I did. No. It isn't the same. John knew he could share anything with me. I tried my best to be the kind of mother I'd always wanted and never had. I always told John that he was the best thing that ever came into my life, no matter what."

"You can't be a mind reader. You couldn't have predicted what John was planning, but it helps to understand if your personalities and your responses to stress were similar."

Mary didn't accept my explanation. "His demons were different from mine. If I'd had his drive when I was eighteen, I could have stood up to my mother. I wouldn't have had to do something stupid like take a bunch of pills!"

"Mary, did John ever tell you that he felt different, not like everyone else? Or did you ever think he was uncomfortable with being different from his peers?"

Mary smiled. "You're describing me now, Doctor, not John. John was insecure, and he needed a lot of stroking. When he was home those last two days, he told me, 'You lied to me when you said I was good-looking. I know that's crap.' He said to me, 'Look at this nose, my skin, you can barely see my beady eyes!' But then he laughed at me. 'It's a face only a mother can love, right?' That's what he said."

"Let's look back at that camping trip again. Why did John decide to go with those boys? It seems so odd, at that time of year, when it's so cold, and the weather is so unpredictable."

"No, not really. John was a Boy Scout working for Eagle Scout and he loved camping. He used to go every year in March. Actually, it was me who wanted him to go with a group of guys. These guys were going to be counselors at an Outward Bound Program, so they wanted John to give them some tips."

Mary once again recited the events preceding John's death: "When I came home from work, he was sitting in his bathrobe, watching TV. He said he wasn't feeling well; first couple of days he was home, and then he went to school just for the morning. He saw one of the guys from the trip, got into an argument with him. Someone said he punched him, but I still have a hard time believing that. The next thing he must have done was to go out and buy a gun. That was in the afternoon, and the next morning he killed himself."

She took a deep breath and went on: "When we found John, the song 'Die Young, Stay Beautiful' was playing on his stereo. What does that say? He cared about his looks so much. What if his face had been blown off? Was he afraid he might not die and what then? We watched a show on TV once about some boys who were stoned, listening to some awful music, and then one of them shot his face off and survived. What a hell that was for him! He looked so repulsive, like someone in a horror movie. John was shaken up by that show, I'll tell you. Not for John! No way! He wouldn't take that chance. The gun he used was almost foolproof. Of course, a foolproof gun."

"Did you ever find out what the fight at school was about?"

"You asked me that before. I told you there was nothing anyone could tell me!"

"Mary, something happened on the camping trip that pushed John over the edge. I think you do know what it was, and frankly I think it's torturing you. Maybe you're still not ready to talk about it. Maybe it's too hard. But when you're ready, there's nothing so terrible that you can't say it to me in this room."

Mary lowered her eyes: "Listen, you remember I said that John had girlfriends, didn't I? He wasn't a ladies man, but he did go out with girls." She was trying very hard to reassure me, reassure herself. "He was no fairy, I'm telling you."

She bit her lip and went on: "I'm trying to tell you that that rotten lying little bastard told me that John came on to him on that camping trip! I'm trying to tell you that he told me John wrote him a love letter. He had the nerve to tell me that on the phone. He even acted like he was the victim. He said the camping trip had been horrible for him because John was coming on to him. John wasn't even around to defend himself. It's impossible! John was straight as an arrow. The counselor at school told me the day John went to school this boy and his friend called him a queer and asked if he was going to queer university. They laughed at him and he just blew up. Can you blame him?"

The atmosphere in the room was electric. Mary herself was stunned at her revelations and looked at me expectantly for my reaction. Before I could say anything, she continued: "Are you satisfied now? I've said it. I've told you what I didn't want to even think. I couldn't even say this to myself. John knew he was gay. My son knew he was not normal. I can't think what's worse: that he was gay, that he was gay and killed himself because of it, or that everyone knows he was gay. But what does it matter. He's dead."

"Could you have accepted it if you'd known he was gay?"

"No way, no way. I wish I could say it doesn't matter to me, especially now because he's dead, but it does. I think that life is the worst, the absolute worst." She shuddered at the very thought.

At the end of our meeting, Mary told me that having no son was better than having a gay son, and that this was an unalterable belief, a part of her personality. She saw me for two more meetings, during which time we together explored this attitude and how it had dominated her perception of John's death. She regretted having this attitude toward homosexuality, which may have been inadvertently conveyed to her son. With time and patience she might have accepted him as a homosexual. It didn't matter; he never gave her that painful choice to make.

Perhaps another explanation is worth considering. John may have had a passing homosexual attraction to another classmate. Many adolescents experiment with homosexuality without remaining homosexual forever. The reaction to John's homosexual "advance" was so intolerant and unaccepting that he could never forgive himself. He felt the need to punish himself for what he did. Indeed, John's intolerance reminded me of Mary's.

■ ■ ■

Many factors increase one's risk for suicide: panic, anxiety, a family history of depression, homosexuality, unrealistic standards, and intolerable rigidity. To varying degrees John experienced each one of these; he chose suicide to shut off the resulting pain. More than any other factor, perhaps his rigidity and intolerance drove him to suicide. He could not accept his homosexual urges and sat in judgment on himself and decided he should not live any longer. With counseling, could John have accepted his homosexual behavior? Rather than see life in simple black-and-white terms, could he have accepted the various shades of gray that characterize human beings? Could Mary also have become less intolerant and rejecting? At the very least, John must have feared rejection by the most important person in his life, his mother.

Part of John's rigid, uncompromising view of himself relates to being young and inexperienced. As we mature, we understand that people are very complex and cannot be simply compartmentalized or characterized as being all one thing or another. Perhaps his suicide may also be a reflection on our times, when some young people view homosexuality so negatively that they would rather choose death.

Mary Pacelli's history of having made a serious suicide attempt suggests a vulnerability to extreme solutions which may have been passed on to her son. Suicide does, indeed, run in families. Would it have helped if John had known about his mother's suicide attempt? Is sharing this history the same as providing a sanctioned role model, thereby encouraging suicidal behavior? It is my feeling that children should be told about a parent's suicide attempt, but in the right way. It is important for adolescents to know that when they get depressed they may have a tendency toward self-destruction, like their parent. They should be taught to recognize self-destructive urges and to immediately talk to someone and get help. Reacting to stress with a suicide attempt didn't help their parents; nor would it help them. If John had been forewarned that when he felt very depressed he had to become aware of suicidal tendencies and go for help, he might be alive today.

"BOYS WILL BE BOYS"

In most cases referred to me for the study on adolescent suicide, the individual was or could have been diagnosed with depression, bipolar (manic-depressive) disorder, or schizophrenia. Frequently drug and/or alcohol abuse was a contributing but not causative factor in the suicide. Many of the youth I have studied experimented with drugs, but more significantly, also had a diagnosable psychiatric illness. Their drug use seemed a function of their efforts to self-medicate the symptoms of the underlying disorder. They used cocaine or amphetamines to elevate their mood when they were depressed and alcohol to temper the mood swings of mania or the pain of anxiety. There were few "pure" substance abusers. Instead, most were what psychiatrists call "dually diagnosed"; that is, they had two psychiatric illnesses: one non-drug-related; the other a substance abuse disorder.

David Collins, aged twenty-three, killed himself nearly ten years before I began work on the suicide study. He shot himself in the heart a few yards from his parents' home. The coroner's report showed that he had taken a large quantity of drugs and drunk at least 16 ounces of whiskey in a four-hour period before his death. Although the official cause of death was a gunshot wound to the heart, we have to ask whether he would have shot himself had he not been so intoxicated.

David's family was devoutly Roman Catholic. Clare, his mother, and Don, his father, were both second-generation Irish-American. Don was the only one in his family to have completed college. He had worked days and attended school at night for more than twelve years, until he earned an M.A. in education. He had worked his way up to become vice principal at an inner-city junior high school. Clare raised their four children, and when the youngest entered high school, she returned to work in a large local department store. David was their second child. Kim was his older sister, Chris the younger brother, and Mary Pat the youngest.

Clare and Don contacted me on the advice of their parish priest, Father Hannah, who was working with me regarding a difficult psychiatric case in the diocese. Although in many ways Clare and Don thought they had long ago worked through David's death, for reasons unclear to them they had recently been suffering from anxiety, grief reactions, and doubts. Father Hannah believed it was related to the suicide ten years earlier and encouraged them to meet with me.

Clare and Don, now in their late fifties, resembled one another, like many couples who have been married for a long time. Both were of average height. Don's brush-cut, flecked with gray, still had some signs of the red it once was. He was dressed in a worn navy blazer that had seen better days, school pin attached to his lapel. Clare, dressed in a conservative formal suit, had not a wrinkle in her creamy skin. With an inquiring arched eyebrow in my direction, Don pulled out a pipe and tobacco from a beaten leather pouch. I nodded that it was all right to smoke.

The Collinses had had no professional assistance in dealing with David's suicide, other than counseling with their priest in the weeks immediately following his death. Our first meeting began awkwardly. Clare seemed particularly wary of speaking. Don explained their reluctance.

"I'm not really sure why we're here today, except that Father Hannah wanted us to come. Maybe he thinks it's your turn to exorcise our devils. Clare and I haven't been ourselves for a while now—Padre thinks it's because we've been brooding a lot about David. I'm not sure what good talking about it now can do." They looked at each other, fumbling for words.

I asked them: "Do you agree with Father Hannah?"

Clare cleared her throat, and began. "Dr. Slaby, do you know anything about us, about David?"

I indicated no. She went on, "David was just twenty-three when he died. He had been in the army, stationed in Manila. He picked up malaria during his second year in the service, and when it didn't get better they sent him home. They weren't even sure if he had any brain damage. Medical care over there was awful, so we never got the whole story. We think there were a whole lot of reasons for his suicide: his girlfriend broke up with him the week after he got back; he came back from Manila on drugs, no better than a street addict—marijuana, heroin, cocaine, he took them all; and he drank a lot."

"Were you aware of whether he used drugs before he went over?"

"Well, I guess you never really know what your kids are doing, do you? I knew he drank, as boys do, but I don't know if he ever took drugs."

Don took a long puff on his pipe. In the smoky haze from his pipe, he signaled to me that he wanted to say something.

"I always figured it had to be a few things, not one problem alone, you know? At the beginning, we looked back at the weeks before he died over and over. I asked myself, should I have seen it coming? Did he ever say something about suicide to me? I didn't remember anything like that. He was on so many drugs, drank a lot of whiskey, too, that's what it said in the coroner's report."

Clare added, "David was on one hundred percent disability from the service because of a brain infection that he got with the malaria. You know, he was in a coma for five days in Manila and they thought he would die. It was a miracle that he didn't. A miracle from God. He was supposed to go for physical therapy three times a week, but he stopped going because he said it didn't help. And David, well, he was always a rebel and that didn't help either."

"What do you mean—rebel? What was he like as a boy, before he went into the army?"

Clare described David without giving it a moment's thought, mechanically; she had made this speech many times—to her priest, to her husband, and, most likely, to herself. I wondered if she'd modified her impressions with the years: "From the time he was a little boy, he was determined, set in his ways, and hyperactive—that's what my doctor said. I used to joke that he was active from the minute I got pregnant." Clare blushed, as though she'd revealed some intimacy reserved for only the closest of friends. "You know what I mean. Rules were for other kids, his sisters, and Chris. He saw things his way, and when everyone else didn't agree he'd get real upset. The drugs—that was unbelievable for all of us, and he knew it, but he couldn't stop. He was so, so frustrated, so cranky all the time. I've had ten years to think about it. I don't think anyone could have talked him out of killing himself; no one even had the chance. He even chose a way that wouldn't fail. He shot himself. Boom, over, done with. David was a hunter, a soldier. He knew how to use a gun."

Young people aspire to unrealistic expectations; that's part of growing up. When anxiety and depression develop when someone does not live up to his or her own ideals, psychologists say there is a difference between the ideal self and the real self. To what degree did David's inability to achieve his ideals contribute to the suicide? Clare described David's response to disappointment. "He would get into a deep, dark funk if things didn't go the way he thought they should. If he had to change his plans in any way or something with his girlfriend didn't go right, oh what a big deal it would become. He was never satisfied with the way things were going, even when they seemed fine. It drove us all crazy."

"Were there any major disappointments?"

Clare began, "I have to think about that . . . it's been so long. He expected everyone to go out on a limb the same way he did. Not only us, his sisters, Chris, but his friends, too. He was a very loyal person about everything. He would give the shirt off his back to anyone who needed it; like if some boy had a fight with his parents, David would bring him home." Don took Clare's hand as she spoke; he sensed that her reserve was beginning to falter. "David was so hurt when he realized everyone wasn't like that. Like some of his friends he made in the service, they didn't stay in touch with him once they got back."

Don nodded as she spoke; "Clare's right. One of the things that really disappointed me was that hardly any of his friends bothered to come around after he died. Only one or two stayed in touch with us. He was such a good friend to them. I don't know if they felt responsible, maybe guilty, because they were all doing drugs together. Did they know he was planning to kill himself? Did they know something we didn't? I don't know."

Most suicides are precipitated by the interaction of a number of factors, particularly in someone genetically predisposed to depression, schizophrenia, anxiety, or impulsivity. Drugs and alcohol decrease judgment and increase impulsivity. In a depressed person drug and/or alcohol addiction can be deadly. Even if a person does not consciously consider suicide, an "accident" can occur under the influence. An intoxicated person inadvertently is directed to his or her death by risk-taking behaviors, an overdose, or a single car accident.

At the end of our first session, I began to construct a hypothesis about the risk factors that may have converged to cause David to take his own life: drug and alcohol abuse; a fairly inflexible temperament; a sensitive, chronically depressed, rigid personality. There were more questions I needed to pursue. When did the drug use begin? Why did his relationship with his girlfriend end?

The next time we met, I explained to Don and Clare that I wanted to concentrate on some of the larger issues that had come up shortly before David's death. I began by asking about David's drug use. Don remembered and explained to me: "Chris, David's brother, told us David had used marijuana before he went to the Philippines, and of course over there, all kinds of drugs were around—cheap, too. That's where he really got into the heroin and cocaine. All his buddies used drugs over there, mainly because they were so bored and lonely."

"Why did he go into the service?"

"He wanted to get a profession. His grades were not great. He knew he'd never get a scholarship or get into a decent college. The army would be his ticket to college. Lots of kids in our neighborhood get their education like that. But he hated the army; his letters about the army were awful. He was really disillusioned. David was so patriotic—it was a real shock for him and for us."

David's world changed after his army experience. According to his parents, before he left he was fanatic about things being organized. Things had to be done a certain way, the food on his plate couldn't touch, clothes in his closet were lined up by color. But it was only one side of his personality. At school he was the opposite, disorganized; his work was usually handed in late and he didn't seem to care.

David had a number of other problems as a child that may have impaired his ability to handle stress as an adult. "He was hyperactive, that's what the pediatrician told me. From the time he was a baby he was on the move all the time." Clare smiled at the memory. "He was very small when he was born, puny but long, and he just sort of grew into a puny tall adult. I'm Rh negative, but he was the only one of our kids who had any problems with the Rh factor when he was born. At first we were afraid he wouldn't make it, but oh, was he feisty! He must have known life would be hard for him."

Clare Collins never thought about David as being depressed. On the contrary, she remembered how he would act out "to get everything out of his system. He would blow up at the drop of a hat and ten minutes later it was all over. Everyone else was still mad at him, but he was acting like nothing had happened."

Clare looked up. "But you know, I think something else, maybe somebody else, was mixed up in his suicide. Long ago I figured out that his decision to commit suicide had something to do with the fact that he was dealing drugs. Anyone who's into drugs has to have a way to support it and we wouldn't pay, that's for sure. He had a disability check from the government, some state unemployment benefits, and he worked part-time. So he had money. We took a little bit for room and board, not much, but mainly kept it in a savings account in David's name. Tuesday morning before David died some guy called him, said he'd better help him move some drugs or he'd give his name to the police. We put it together after he died. David must have panicked. He seemed very, very afraid and at the last minute wouldn't help this guy, because he was convinced he would get caught."

"How soon after that did he kill himself?"

"The next morning."

Over time, and with input from interviews with some of David's friends, I learned that despite Clare's feelings to the contrary David was using speed long before joining the army. Together, we reconstructed the night before he killed himself: He was up all night, feverishly writing. Later they found his suicide notes to each family member and his letters of good-bye to his friends. He got the energy to write them after bingeing on large doses of amphetamines. Once he "crashed" from the effects of the speed, he began drinking, became morose, and in a post-stimulant depression, shot himself.

Clare said, "We found this pile of papers, a shoe box full of ripped up and crumpled messages. You know, he would write something and if it wasn't what he wanted to say, tear it up. Finally, at the end, the last note that he wrote was the one that he left us. The felt-tip marker was running out of ink, it was so faded. You could just see the frustration—even the damn pen wouldn't cooperate for him."

Clare had brought David's suicide note with her to the session. She asked if she could read it. It was addressed to the whole family:

*I hope you understand that this is the best.
All I've ever done is screw up my whole life.
My mind is no longer my own, it seems.
Everything I touch goes bad.
    P.S. Things like this often bring a family
closer together.*

"Was your family having problems when David killed himself?" I asked. Clare stared off into space for a while, and then turned toward me as she answered, "Not then—none that we couldn't work out." Don was sitting across from me, blowing smoke rings into the air with his pipe. It was irritating to me, and I regretted allowing him to smoke. The pipe was becoming his diversion, leaving Clare to do most of the work.

"Did David ever get psychiatric help?"

"When he was in high school I found appointment slips in his pants pockets from a school counselor. And he said that he was seeing someone at the Veterans Hospital for counseling after he got back from Manilla."

As with other suicides, David's death was rooted in complicated issues. True, he was severely depressed after crashing from speed and he was frightened about the consequences of his selling drugs. But his friends had said there were problems in his relationship with his girlfriend, Rose. I asked Don to tell me about Rose.

"Rose and David dated during his senior year. She was great for him, made him laugh. I liked her a lot. Rose comes from a strict family where they always know what she's doing, where she's going. Her parents never liked David because he was so independent, and they thought he was not respectful enough. One night her dad smelled marijuana in the house and he threw David out. They snuck around to see each other after that, but it was never the same. When he came back from the army, Rose was in nursing school, and she said she wasn't going to waste time on him unless he stopped all drugs, alcohol, the works. In his last note to her, he said something like 'I can't stop drugs, but I can't lose you.' "

From the time I had first met the Collinses I wondered what caused them now, after so many years, to have second thoughts about David's suicide. When I asked, Don shifted in his seat. He took his leather tobacco pouch from the table and nervously lit his pipe. I noticed that his hands were shaking.

Clare, seeing his discomfort, spoke up a little too quickly, not very convincingly: "This Saturday would have been David's birthday. He killed himself a week after his birthday. Every year these days are very hard for Don, for us. It's easier now than it was at the beginning, but each year as we get older, we think about what might have been. Sometimes when you least expect it, it bothers you. David didn't go to church much, but he did believe in God, and he loved to sing at church. In the weeks before he died he would hum a hymn, my mother's favorite hymn. It reminded both of us of my mother, who had lived with us. Now I hate the song. I just can't hear it. I swear, I hear that song everywhere. It drives me up a tree. Maybe that's what's doing it—we're getting older, and it's not getting better."

I had in mind one more question, referring to David's postscript about people getting closer together after a suicide, but I stopped myself. I felt some unspoken tension, something troubling. Maybe we had probed enough that day. It would have to wait.

At our next meeting, the two daughters, Kim and Mary Pat, joined their parents. Each had brought some letters David had written to them from Manila, as well as the last notes he had written them the night before his suicide. We spent some time reading the letters. His suicide notes to them were not unlike the letter he'd written to Clare and Don, but he added a special note to his nieces and nephews, telling them that they had given him the most pleasure in his life. His parents had never read their letters. They seemed to tune out while we talked and were relieved when I turned to them and asked if they had any questions.

Don began: "I forgot to ask last time, but I wondered, is it possible for someone to decide to kill himself if he hears about someone else, maybe a famous person, who died from an overdose? David died maybe six or eight weeks after two rock stars—I forget their names—died that way."

Another contributing factor had spontaneously come up.

I nodded, "There definitely can be a relationship between a high-profile death by suicide and imitating behavior. In fact, the number of suicide attempts and completions rises after the news breaks. Kids may identify with the star, or they see it as a way of calling attention to themselves. Suicide becomes romanticized when a famous person's life is splashed across the TV news. Even if David had never considered suicide before that, in his depressed state after taking all those drugs and alcohol, he became more vulnerable."

I was about to ask Kim and Mary Pat if they had anything they'd like to share about David's suicide when Don interrupted to apologize for the absence of Chris, David's brother. "In some ways Chris needs to be here more than anyone else. Chris has never been the same since David died."

Kim spoke up, looking directly at her parents, "I don't think everyone is being honest here. I said I would come only if you told the truth. The real problem is that Chris has been on drugs for years. He's been depressed, and I'm sure he's thought about suicide. And you—after all that's happened you should be honest about it!"

Don and Clare were silent, their eyes focused on the poster on the wall, the stacks of magazines on the table. They wouldn't look at her or me directly.

"Chris was having problems at work and kept to himself most of the time. But he's not a kid—what the hell could I do?" Clare's voice rose as she responded to Kim. I looked over at Don. He was thumbing through some books on the shelves, trying very hard not to be part of this conversation. I turned to him.

"Don, what was your relationship with Chris and David like?"

Kim and Mary Pat exchanged triumphant smiles. Something was going on. Don ran his fingers through his stubby brush-cut, adjusted his belt, shifted in his seat. "Here's the part where I get beat up. Right, girls? No, we didn't get along at all, the boys were always mad at me, said I gave more time, more every-thing, to my students than to them. But it wasn't true. Problem is, I work in a school where most of the guys have no father, so I'm it. I couldn't even mention any of these kids, or their prob-lems at home, especially in front of the boys."

Mary Pat was flipping through David's last notes: "I feel so guilty about David. I'm always the one my friends come to when they have a problem. And I couldn't even help my own brother. I keep thinking that when he was reaching out, I wasn't there. But neither were my parents. They've never been honest with themselves, certainly not with us. They act like we're like the family in 'Father Knows Best.' It's never been like that, never."

Clare stood up and stared at Mary Pat with loathing. "Shut the hell up. What right have you got to say those kinds of things? In the name of God what have we ever done to you to deserve this kind of nonsense?" Mary Pat was sobbing uncon-trollably now. Her sister came over to comfort her.

"And don't the two of you act so injured. Haven't we always made sure you had a home, an education? Who lived with us for six months when her husband was out of work? Did we ever take a penny from you? No. And you"—pointing at Kim—"how can you look at me with that hate? When you were pregnant and didn't want that baby, who didn't interfere when you got an abortion? You know what that was like for me? Did we ever throw your brothers out when they were taking drugs, when we thought David was working with that dealer, that scum? No, we just looked the other way."

Kim shouted back: "That's just it, you looked the other way. You went to church every day and said those fucking masses, and took your beads out, pretended we were this normal happy family, but did you do anything? Did you ever ask why? You even accepted Dad's horrible perverted behavior. That was the worst. Why do you think we're all so messed up now? Nothing will take that away, not church, not God, not candles, nothing!"

The room was silent, absolutely silent. But the fury that had been unleashed remained suspended in the air. Mary Pat regained her composure, and went on, "It has to be told, mother, it has to. David was killing himself in your house since high school. You know that. He went into the army to get out of our loony bin. Each of us ran away. And we're all paying for it now. Tell them, Dad, tell them, about your honorable life."

Clare walked over to the door. "I won't sit here and take this any more. I'm leaving now. Don, are you coming?"

"Wait, Clare, we have to talk this out, this is no good, don't leave."

Clare stormed out of the office. Don snatched their coats from the sofa and ran after her.

I sat there facing the two women: "That must have been very hard for you. Have you ever confronted them before like that?" Kim couldn't look at me. She covered her face with her hands. Mary Pat, realizing that she had forced some painful issues into the open, answered.

"Look, Dr. Slaby, I didn't want to come here because I knew this would happen. I knew that talking about David would cause the truth to come out. It's not like he took drugs, crashed, and died. It's not like that. My mother likes to say he was always a rebel but it was worse than that. He was like someone who had demons inside him, telling him what to do."

Kim snickered at the analogy. "Now you sound like the nuns at school."

Mary Pat went on: "You know what I mean, Kim. David used to come to school stoned, if he came to school at all. Oh sure, he left the house, even took his books with him, but half the time he never got there. And that part about him always needing things a certain way, that was only at home, it was his way of running my mother, all of us, in circles."

"Didn't your parents know—I mean about the drugs, school, all of that?"

"They did and they didn't. They were having their own problems, my dad was, anyway. They were thrilled when David went into the army because he'd be gone and someone else could supervise him. But it just became worse in the army because of the drugs and the drinking. Maybe if he hadn't gone to Manila, but no, it wouldn't have mattered. Oh, I'm sorry, I just remembered—I drove us all here. I've got to find my parents and take them home. Can we make an appointment to see you alone? I guess you've figured out there's a lot of things you should know about."

It was an ominous close to a trying session. I wanted to hear more. I was more than merely curious about what event might lurk in the past. I could only speculate about the festering obstacles to emotional well-being in the Collins family.

I had some time to look over David's suicide notes, which his parents and sisters had left behind in their rush. Suicide notes hardly eliminate the grief for survivors, but David's passionate notes, like so many others I have read, gave me some insight into the intense suffering and irrational state of mind that precede a suicide. The importance of a note in providing some answers, no matter how disjointed, to the consuming question "Why?" cannot be minimized.

> *I'm really sorry it had to end this way but I love you too much too much to be without you. This really is the only way I'll ever find any peace or be happy. So please don't anyone be sad.*

He had convinced himself that by ending his own life his parents would be less burdened and could repair their own shattered lives.

Kim called the next morning to set up an appointment. As she told the secretary, "If I don't do this now, I'm afraid I'll become like my parents, and I couldn't stand that." Her sister wouldn't be coming, she added, because she was "a basket case" after the last session.

Kim was half an hour early for our appointment. She was sitting in the hall munching a sandwich and juggling a cup of coffee when I came out of the office. "I know I'm early. I could have been here at six in the morning, I'm so wired."

"Have you spoken to your parents at all? We tried calling them but they didn't call back. Do you know if they want to continue these meetings?"

She shrugged her shoulders. "My mother refuses to speak to either of us since we met with you. I'm not surprised, but I'm not worried either. She'll get over it. This isn't the first time she's refused to talk with us. That's always been her way of controlling us. When we were younger, we'd always give in and apologize, beg forgiveness when she got that mad. When we were little kids she would pretend that we didn't exist when she was mad at us. She always said it was better than hitting us, or screaming at us. I think it was worse."

"Tell me, Kim, at our last meeting, you made it clear that there were some things I should know. Are you ready to talk about them?"

"There are a few things." Kim took a deep breath. "I'm going to start with Chris, because that's easier. About a week before David died, Chris was very cruel to him. I remember it clearly because it was Easter Sunday, and we were all together at my parents' house for supper. They nearly punched each other. And it was Chris who started it. He just picked at David, pick, pick pick, you know what I mean?"

"Did they usually get along?"

"They were really close until Chris got married. Growing up we all stuck together because it was so hard growing up in that house. But when David came back from the service he was so weird he got on everyone's nerves. It was worse for Chris because his marriage had broken up, and I think he hoped he and David would live together, and things would be like when they were kids."

"You say David was weird. How?"

"He would sleep all day and prowl around at night; he looked messy, didn't care about what he wore or how he looked. First my dad was after him to go to physical therapy; then he was on his case about getting a job, anything to get him out of the house. I knew he was dealing drugs, and when I'd ask him to get some help, he would ignore me. What else? Oh, he spent most of his time in his room, drawing, playing solitaire, eating junk food. And it was like the rest of us were just not part of his life. Chris really felt rejected, angry."

As Kim went on, I had a sense of the blaming common in so many families.

"Right after he died—you know he shot himself in my dad's car, parked in the driveway?" I nodded. "My parents were blaming each other. My father was furious that both my mother and Chris knew that David had a gun but he didn't know. I don't think it would have made any difference if he knew, but for a long time it was a big deal between them. A lot of other things were flying back and forth that made things worse. And they had mostly to do with the fact that—and this is another thing I know no one's told you—my dad had mental problems for years. I know you didn't know that. I don't know if Father Hannah knows, but we sure did."

"Was your dad ever hospitalized?"

"I think he had shock treatment when we were in high school—does that sound right? He would be away for a few weeks, usually after some big blowup with my mother. I remember thinking it was weird that my mother never went to see him, but she always said he needed some rest, or it was too hard on her, whatever that meant. We didn't ask, none of us did. When he came back, he'd be tired, spacey for a while, and then he'd be better—until the next time."

"How often did that happen?"

"I knew you'd ask a lot of questions I couldn't answer. Aren't we supposed to talk about David? Never mind." She sighed deeply. "My dad had an affair. My mother told me about it once, one of the times he was away having his brain fried or whatever they did there. It was just before I graduated high school. I came home real late and she was alone in the kitchen, crying. I never saw my mother cry except at funerals, and even then she could turn it on and off, depending on who she thought was watching. She was rambling on about her life and how God was always testing her. Dad had an affair with a secretary at his school. It didn't last long, I think only weeks, and he was real weepy about it, she said. He blamed it on being depressed."

"How much did David know about the affair or the hospitalization?"

Kim looked down at her long thin fingers. For a moment she appeared transfixed by one of her crimson nails. When she looked up at me, she was crying, "Oh God, I hate talking about this!"

"I'm not in a rush. I can wait until you're ready. Would you like anything to drink?" She shook her head and opened up her pocketbook, fumbling inside it until she found a newspaper clipping, which she put on my desk. As I reached over, she put one of my books on top of the clipping, "Please, don't read that now. Wait until I leave." She continued.

"I was the one who told David, Mary Pat, Chris about the affair. Why wouldn't I? Wouldn't you? But there was something else, something worse." She took a deep breath, cleared her throat several times, and waited a moment before resuming, "My dad was accused by two guys in his class, students David's age, of . . . of coming on to them. They said he hugged them and twice tried to kiss them. Oh God, they made it sound was like my dad was a pervert! Dad denied it. He said these boys needed a dad and he was reaching out to them. We were all so ashamed. There was a closed hearing, at the school board, but only my parents went. He told the board he was trying to be a father figure, that these kids were practically on the street. In the end they put him on medical leave for six months, because he'd been getting help."

"Is that what the clipping is about?"

Kim nodded, "After David came back from Manila, Dad applied for a promotion, and then, somehow, it came out, even though it was all settled long before."

"How did it affect the family?"

"At first, David and Chris, neither of them, could face my dad. They just pretended it never happened. David did drugs more, drank a lot, stayed in his room, drew these horrible post-

ers, awful pictures of people with knives to their throat, with
guns, I couldn't even stand to see them. I tossed them after he
died, they were just too frightening. David blamed himself completely for Dad's problems. He told Chris—me too—if he had
been a better son, if he didn't get into drugs and screw up his
life, Dad wouldn't have needed to be a father to those boys. Our
family wouldn't be in the mess it was. He wanted us to be a
family, for once."

"Are you saying that's one of the reasons he killed himself?
That he convinced himself he was responsible for his dad's
behavior?"

"Look at David's note, where he said sometimes these things
bring a family closer together. I mean, doesn't that tell you
something? It's awful to say, but in a way he was right, his
dying did help pull us all together, just like he said it would."

"Your dad is a vice principal now?"

"Well, he didn't get the job he applied for that time, but he
wasn't a criminal. When he was up for another job, a couple of
school districts away, he got it. So big deal, who the hell cares
about a promotion now? His son's dead."

Kim had trouble understanding her father's behavior, particularly since he had always been distant with his own children.
His emotional problems had never been talked about within the
family. Kim seriously doubted that even her mother understood
what was wrong with Don. When asked, Clare would only say,
"He can't help himself. He's a good man. Pray, if you want to
help your father."

I wanted to believe that in the more than ten years since
David Collins had killed himself, ignorant attitudes, silence, and
fear, especially on the subject of mental illness, would have les-
sened. On the surface, the Collins family, through their reliance
on religious faith, their pride, and perhaps an amazing capacity
for denial, had remained intact. Clare had learned to live with
Don's problems and David's death without understanding
either the illness or any possible connection, father to son. From
time to time, Kim had allowed herself to express anger and to

question. But, a decade later, she, too, was no wiser. Chris, a substance abuser, chronically depressed, remained a vulnerable and problematic adult.

I very much wanted to meet with Don and Clare Collins at least once more. Clare refused to connect again, reasoning that it would not be helpful. But Don came to see me one last time. As we sat down together, I saw how intently Don looked at my face, checking for approval or disapproval. I felt enormously sad for him. Initially, we spoke about more neutral issues, such as how Clare was doing since the last traumatic session. I suggested psychiatric referrals for both Clare and for Chris. And then Don, acknowledging the difficulties he'd had over the years and referring repeatedly to the issues Kim had raised, described his guilt over his failure to communicate with David and the damage his fumbling attempts at closeness with his students had caused.

"The worst thing that bothered me after David died was that we had never really been close. We were always arguing about school, his attitude, grades, all of it. Every day I work with kids who have nothing. David had everything and he threw it away long before he killed himself. That's what I resented the most, I admit it. I let him know, too. Maybe I shouldn't have."

Don was reflective in talking about the reasons David committed suicide. "It's so much easier for us to say it was drugs, the army, Rose. We could kind of put each thing in its own compartment, you know what I mean? He was never the same when he came back from Manila."

I asked, "Don, do you see any connection between your depressions years ago, the shock treatments, and David's problems?"

"You think I'm surprised by that question, don't you? Well I'm not. I'm not surprised at all. That's what was so scary for me—I saw me, I saw David, and then Chris, and we were all the same. David, Chris, me, the three musketeers; I just didn't want to think that I could have done that to my boys. The girls are like Clare—bitchy, tough, hard as nails. But the boys are like me, putty. Except I promised to never let my boys have those shock treatments. They were hell. Like how they treated crazies in the Middle Ages. Oh sure, I'd be better for a while after. But I had no choice. They had a choice."

"What was that?"

"The army, the school counselor, social workers; everyone has a shingle nowadays. Hey, they could have come to me. I didn't have anyone I could talk to. But they would never come to me."

"If there was anything you could have done differently, what would it be?"

Don seemed to be talking to himself for a while, thinking about my question. "Well, I guess I would have tried harder to be there for them, even when they put me off. I would've hung in there for them, been there for them in spite of their trying to push me away. And I wouldn't have had that affair, even though, let me tell you, it was a lot better for me than shock treatment."

■　■　■

From David Collins's suicide we learn how complex and multi-determined the decision to take one's own life may be. David was genetically predisposed to depression. Other members of his family had problems, particularly his father. David was a substance abuser, which decreased his judgment and increased his impulsivity. No one involved in David's life could distinguish between his despair and his abuse of chemicals. The self-medication not only alleviated his own inner anguish but also clouded the symptoms of depression.

David struggled with long-standing conflict with his father. His identification with his father troubled him greatly. He viewed his dad as someone who had recurrent depressions and very poor impulse control. His affair with the secretary and the incidents with the students confirmed David's impression that his father was weak. The family did not cope well with the father's problems and Chris's and David's substance abuse. They were unable to tackle these problems head-on and address them in an effective manner. It was too overwhelming. David did not allow anyone to help him. In David's mind, asking for help was the ultimate sign of weakness. Acknowledging and getting treatment for his depression would have been an indication that he was like his father.

This family lived with a number of secrets that exerted undue control over the family members. It would have been so helpful to discuss the father's recurrent depressions, affair, and pedophilic advances openly and honestly. Instead, the secrets weighed heavily on all their minds and ultimately destroyed David. Revelation might have provided relief and respite.

"IT WASN'T SUICIDE, IT WAS MURDER"

To My Friends,

God could not have given me any better friends than he did and I thank Him for it.

Tim

Teachers, counselors, psychologists, psychiatrists—we all ask the same questions as parents when a child chooses to end his or her life: Could we have done anything differently? Did we ignore some obvious clue? We assume that somehow we failed; we did not act effectively in behalf of that child.

This is particularly true when professionals—teachers, coaches, health or social service providers—come in contact with children who they know or strongly suspect have been abused. Most feel frustration and anger at their inability to rescue these children from sexual, physical, and emotional abuse. Much like children who have been abused, children who have severe depression are isolated, experience terrible feelings of worthlessness, and cannot seem to access or benefit from professional help. It is not surprising, then, that the literature on child abuse documents a strong relationship between abuse and depression and suicide.

Professionals are frequently asked to provide testimony and

recommendations in cases of young children and teens who have been abused. These children are often severely depressed and at risk for self-destructive behavior. Their family problems are usually chronic and often complicated by weaknesses in the service delivery system. These weaknesses include the inability, for many reasons, to adequately follow up on suspected victims of abuse; general suspicion on the part of families of any outside treatment; and a pervasive attitude among professionals that abusive families (particularly if the parents are poor, teenage, or belong to a minority group) are not responsive to treatment. Irrespective of their training and experience and what they may perceive to be an even-handed, family-based therapeutic approach, mental health professionals are considered by some families to be harsh and judgmental.

Incidents of physical, sexual, and emotional abuse are inex-cusable and traumatic violations of children's rights; moreover, without skilled intervention, child and adolescent victims become re-victimized. The long-term effects of consistent abuse are incalculable, but studies routinely include delinquency, sub-stance abuse, promiscuity, eating disorders, as well as a wide range of emotional disturbances.

While physical and sexual abuse can be quantified and catego-rized according to bruises, fractures, burns, rape, pregnancy, and sexually transmitted diseases, emotional and verbal abuse—the pattern of continually undermining and belittling a child through criticism and verbal attacks—is equally damaging and much more insidious. Verbal abuse is more common than either physical or sexual abuse, and yet it is seldom adequately identified or treated. Most often, treatment comes many years later, as adults willingly or unwillingly try to sort out their diffi-cult childhoods. These adults have usually had considerable problems; worse yet, they may be emotionally abusive to their own children. Parents cannot easily be charged with emotional and verbal abuse; interventions by teachers or social workers are often dismissed as overreactions to parenting style. "That's how I grew up and it didn't hurt me at all," or "He's a bad kid. If I don't tell him, who will?" These are common responses from parents, even though more information and classes about positive parenting styles and stress management are generally available. These classes are available to all income groups, in culturally and racially sensitive contexts, and yet emotional and verbal abuse continues to be overwhelmingly difficult to stop or treat.

Tim Morgan was a victim of repeated verbal and emotional abuse. At age sixteen, he killed himself with a single shot to his head, using his father's favorite hunting rifle. He had never before used a gun. He chose to kill himself in back of his house, in full view of his father and his older brother.

Tim was a popular, valued, and respected junior in high school. He had never shown any signs of depression or anxiety. On the contrary, he was a practical joker, a leader in any team sport he attempted. A less than average scholar, Tim was probably college bound on full scholarship because of his sports achievements. College could have been his ticket out of an unhappy home. Unfortunately, he wasn't able to hold out that long.

I had read about Tim's suicide in the papers the next morning, and was not surprised to see a number of messages pertaining to the case on the receptionist's desk when I arrived at the office. I ignored the requests for commentaries by the media, but did respond to a message from a local funeral director.

"Dr. Slaby, my name is John McNally, of McNally Brothers Funeral Chapel. I heard you speak at a seminar on teenage suicide and grief management last year; I really need some advice. I'm calling about Tim Morgan, the boy from Hollins High who killed himself yesterday. His mother, Anna Morgan, came in today with her brother to make arrangements for the funeral. Naturally, she is in terrible shape, says that her son killed himself because he was being emotionally abused by his father. She doesn't want his dad at the funeral. She wants him kept out. On top of that, the newspapers have been calling. I don't want this boy's funeral to be a circus. And I don't want to get in the middle of their problems."

"When have you scheduled the funeral?"

"The day after tomorrow, in the morning."

"Will you be seeing Mrs. Morgan today?"

"I can, but I'm not really sure what fires I should be trying to put out first. I mean, bad family feelings come out when someone dies. That's nothing new, you know—split families, angry great-nieces, people with AIDS whose families ask that no gay people be let into the chapel. We've had to bury other people who killed themselves. We've seen it all. But this is different. I won't let this funeral turn into some kind of trial in front of all those people and the press."

I advised him: "I think the most important thing is to make sure the funeral doesn't become a circus. Spend as much time as possible with Tim's mother, comfort her, and help her see that Tim's funeral needs to be a place where his memory can be respected, can be honored. Tell her there'll be time to talk about her accusations later."

"Should I call the boy's father, and meet with him, and maybe ask him to participate in the funeral?"

"I think you should. And, as for the media, they'll be there, and there's nothing much you can do about that except try to keep them away from the family."

Helga, my secretary, came into the office with another message. One of the guidance counselors from Hollins High was holding on the other line. We knew each other from previous cases we'd worked on together. I took the call.

"Drew, I'm glad I got you. I'm sure you heard about Tim Morgan's death. Tim was an extremely popular student here, active in sports, student council. This isn't a huge high school, so everyone knew him. The kids are just shocked, devastated. Our principal has called an assembly of the sophomore through senior classes at noon today. All the counselors and Tim's teachers will be there too. I'm just getting some materials together about grief, and about suicide. But there's something more troubling about Tim. We've known at the school for a long time that Tim had a terrible relationship with his dad. His friends all knew it too. We didn't, we *couldn't* do anything about it and we all feel terribly responsible. I know it's going to come up in assembly; I just don't know how we're going to respond."

Teachers have often told me that the first meeting with students to talk about a suicide is the most difficult. They themselves have not begun to process their own grief; they themselves are trying to recall their last interaction with the teen. Was it unusual? Did they have any clue? And then they have to face a group of frightened kids who have the same questions. Adolescents are continually struggling with their needs for independence and control, but in the face of tragedy they feel powerless, frustrated, and, above all, vulnerable. So many conflicting raw emotions surface that any responses from adults seem banal and cheap. Tim's friends needed to know that they had not failed him. Like everyone else, and in uniquely adolescent style, they would certainly demand to know why, when it was clear that his home life was so unhappy, no one with more power could have stepped in and prevented this tragedy.

I suggested to him: "I think it's important that you focus the meeting so that you're dealing with their grief and with the concept of suicide as a terrible solution to Tim's frustration and pain. If they want to talk about issues that Tim shared with them privately, they should do so. But if you comment, it will really be a violation of what you heard in confidence from Tim. And you can tell them that. Give them other options. Talk about how they can have a meaningful role in the funeral, suggest that they create some memorial to him, maybe how they could reach out to Tim's mother."

"Will you be at the funeral?"

Before he'd asked the question, I hadn't even thought about attending; I had never met Tim or his family. In some ways it seemed voyeuristic to attend, and yet I sensed that I would probably connect with the family at some time in the future. "I'll have to think about it. What time is it scheduled?"

"It's at noon at McNally's on Franklin."

"I'll do my best."

Sitting in the funeral home the next afternoon, I was gratified to see the number of young people who had come. The chapel was filled to overflowing, and the intrusive cameras and reporters remained outside, so that friends and family could grieve privately. A large picture of Tim stood on an easel near the coffin. It was a candid shot taken on the football field. Tim, his arms extended, was grinning broadly at his teammates.

The minister gave a poignant and brief speech about Tim's strengths, his warm and giving personality, and his skill as an athlete and a team leader. He didn't avoid the issue of Tim's suicide. In fact, he personalized his comments by talking about his own pain when his nephew had killed himself several years earlier. "Tim's death is so troubling for me because in the last few days I have had to finally grieve for my nephew. I had to accept the fact that he chose death and not life. And I had to grieve for the fact that I could not prevent his death because I didn't know . . . I never knew how desperate he was. Grieve for Tim now, not in six months and not in three years, but now. Find out what your friends are really thinking. Are they ever sad? Have they ever thought about or talked about killing themselves? Have they come to anyone for help—a counselor, a doctor, a pastor? Let Tim's legacy be that no other teenager you know ever feels that hopeless again because you will be there for them."

I was glad that the minister had been so open and direct. While he also talked about suicide as a religious taboo, the emphasis was on sending a very clear message to Tim's friends: Suicide should never be an option; there are ways to seek help; there are ways to extend yourself in friendship to someone in need.

Two of Tim's classmates gave very emotional eulogies to their friend; Tim was clearly an unusual and sensitive young man. That year, he had organized a group of students to volunteer as mentors in an inner-city elementary school. For the past two years he had volunteered at a soup kitchen, and ironically, he had talked to his friends about his plans to work at a suicide prevention center once he got to college. Another friend sang a song that had been Tim's favorite, the Beatles' "Yesterday."

As the processional of teenage pallbearers, their tears hidden by sunglasses, slowly inched their way out of the church for the trip to the cemetery, I looked for Tim's family. They came down the aisle first, accompanied by the minister; his mother, father, and a brother who was pushing a very elderly lady in a wheel-chair. The unnatural aspect of Tim's death was reinforced by the presence of this very frail-looking woman, who, I noted as she passed by, was wearing a hospital identification bracelet on her wrist. A day pass to attend a grandchild or great-grandchild's funeral—how many of us would choose to live long enough to be granted that? How many times in the last 48 hours had she asked God why He hadn't taken her instead of Tim?

I didn't accompany the processional to the cemetery. As I drove back to my office, I wondered whether I would hear from Tim's family at all. I thought about Tim, as I do about every young person I read about who has committed suicide. I tried to put the pieces of the puzzle together. Had anyone at the same school committed suicide recently? Had there been any articles in the newspaper or something on TV about suicide?

It was a week before I heard from Tim's mother. When she called, she told me she had been referred by John McNally. I expressed my sympathy about Tim's death. I assumed she needed some help in working through Tim's suicide. But she hadn't called to talk about that.

"Dr. Slaby, I'm calling because I need your help in a divorce action. I'm going to divorce my husband. I have no choice. I should have divorced him years ago. He was the one who really killed Tim. He didn't shoot him, but he might as well have done it himself."

Her voice was constricted because she was breathing so heavily; the more she talked, the more she wheezed. She continued, laboriously: "My husband, Glen, hated Tim from the time he was born. Tim reminded him too much of me—he looked like me; he was very social, like me; he was a leader in sports; he was all the things Glen never was." Anna Morgan was almost whispering now. "I'm having trouble talking—my asthma, the stress. Will you see me?"

Rather than have her talk any longer, I asked Helga to sched-ule an appointment for her as soon as possible. Several days later, there was a faint knock at the office door. Anna Morgan entered the office and introduced herself. "The receptionist isn't at her desk. Is it all right for me to come in now?" The wheezing in her chest was still noticeable. Anna was a petite woman, with long, gray hair tied in a single braid down her back. She was dressed simply and carried a three-ring notebook along with her pocketbook.

Anna sat down facing me across a large coffee table. The wheezing became more pronounced as I told her about my research in suicide, about the pain that exists for parents like herself who lose a child, and about the anger that families carry with them, anger that could easily destroy a marriage.

Anna sat impassively, stroking the notebook on her lap. She flipped through the pages, avoiding any eye contact.

There was a long pause before she spoke: "John McNally spoke to me right after Tim's funeral about coming to see you. He gave me some articles that he got at your class. I've been reading them and can relate to what you're writing. But my case is different. I'm here because I can't live with my husband anymore. If I had left Glen before, I would have taken Tim with me and maybe he would be alive today."

"It sounds like you're blaming yourself for Tim's death."

"Of course I am. Why wouldn't I?"

She went on, "Glen and I got married when we were very young. We only knew each other for a couple of months. He was going to Vietnam, he was scared, he wanted someone in his life. When he left, I was already pregnant with Troy, and when he came back two years later, he decided that he should never have married me. Glen never beat me, like my father did my mother, but he was always on my case . . . always picking on me . . . I wasn't a good housekeeper; I was a lousy mother; I couldn't cook . . . it was always something. Tim was an accident. I didn't even tell him I was pregnant until I was almost five months along. He was furious, said I'd trapped him. So when Tim was born, only I was ready to love him. Only I cared. Never his dad!"

Anna stopped, and took a deep breath. She opened her purse

to get a tissue; the notebook on her lap slid to the floor. Her tears flowed freely.

I asked, "Would you like to rest for a bit?"

Anna nodded, silently. . . . Her hands covered her face completely, and with each heaving sob her whole body convulsed and settled in aching spasms of pain. I left the room to get some water; when I returned, Anna was lying down on the small sofa in my office. She sat up immediately, shaking her head when I offered her the cup.

"I'll be fine . . . I'm used to this," she whispered. "I want to talk about Tim—Tim and his dad. I told you already that Glen never wanted Tim. Glen had set it up so that Tim was my son, and Troy was his. Glen hurt his back in a training accident so he was on disability and was with both kids, sometimes all day for weeks. Troy was always his favorite, even when they were little. He'd always criticize Tim, just like he complained about me."

"Did you ever try to leave him before?"

Anna spoke softly, laboriously: "All my life I looked after the men in my life—first my dad after my mother died, Glen, and then my two boys. If I left, what would I do? Leave them with Glen? No, I couldn't just walk out. Besides, Glen would have given Tim up for adoption. I know it. Once I worked for a while as a waitress, when Tim was just little. I would come home and Glen would be playing with Troy, and Tim would be sitting in his playpen screaming to get out. Then Glen would go on about how awful 'my' boy was, just like he went on about me."

"Did things change at all as Tim was growing up?"

She shook her head. "It got worse. Tim and Glen fought all the time, mainly Glen hammering at him about little things. And the worst part was that Tim never gave him any trouble— never. Lots of times he would just look at Glen, not say a word, just look at him, didn't yell back, cry, nothing."

"Did Glen's abuse affect Tim at school, or with friends?"

"Tim's teachers liked him; he was in Little League, Boy Scouts, soccer. He always had lots of friends. But still, in Glen's mind, he could do nothing right. And Troy could do nothing wrong. I was always getting in between the two of them, trying to make Tim see that I was there for him. I caught hell for it, too, all the time, from Glen. Even Troy hated to watch what was happening to his brother. I know it."

"Tell me about Tim's relationship with Troy."

"I haven't talked about Troy, have I?" She said it almost defensively. "Troy looks just like Glen. He's not tall, like Tim is . . . was . . . or handsome, or athletic. He goes fishing and hunting with his dad. And Troy's an A student. But school was always so hard for Tim. He barely made it through every year. His friends always said the only reason he passed was the teachers liked him so much. Glen used to ride him about that, make fun of him, tell him he was dumb, lazy, a failure. Whenever we would have a fight, he would bring up Tim's grades. But Troy . . . Troy was a good brother to Tim. They weren't close—how could they be when he was Glen's favorite? But he used to step between his dad and Tim when it looked really like they'd . . . they'd punch each other out. Right now he's real confused; he doesn't want to blame Glen, but he's real shaken up. Part of him knows that his dad pushed Tim way too far!"

I could see that Anna was very tired. She reached into her bag and took out her inhaler. A wad of wet tissues tumbled out, along with some loose change, a pocket mirror, a handful of paper scraps and a battered wallet. After a few puffs, she slowly bent down to retrieve her things, and noticed the notebook beneath the chair. With great effort she picked it up, sat up, and handed it to me. "Take a look at this notebook. In English class they were supposed to keep a daily journal. It was in Tim's locker. One of his friends gave it to me at the visitation. I haven't been able to look at it. I take it with me wherever I go, sometimes even in the bathroom, but I can't read it at all. Seeing Tim's handwriting drives me crazy, makes me want to kill Glen, makes me regret every day I spent with him."

I glanced at my watch. There was still fifteen minutes left in the meeting, but I could see that Anna was tired. I agreed to set up three more appointments, and asked Anna if Troy and possibly Glen could be included. Anna was not pleased about including her husband. "I thought you were on my side." I understood her objections, but I had to find out how much of her need to leave the marriage was an immediate reaction to Tim's suicide and how much was her need, finally, to leave an abusive marriage.

When Anna left, I had some time to go through Tim's notebook more thoroughly and to take some detailed notes.

The first revelation did not require much insight: Tim's writing was barely legible and his thoughts seemed nearly incoherent. There was some effort at making the spelling phonetic, but it resembled more the struggles of a young child to write a note than the work of a high school student. There were classic signs of a profound learning disability. Anna had not mentioned whether his school difficulties had ever been diagnosed as a learning disability. She had merely mentioned Glen's conviction that Tim was a lazy and indifferent student. It had been awhile since I had "decoded" such a garbled piece of writing. Most often I would only review samples of written work as part of a comprehensive diagnosis. I read about four or five pages, selecting from the beginning, the middle, and final pages of the notebook. They were irregularly dated; it seemed that most of the entries were made within the last eight months. The randomly selected pages all focused on the duel themes of Glen's hatred of Tim and the comfort Tim found in his friends. One entry:

I hate him so much I could kill him. Today I got my report card. It wasn't any better than last, even worse in math. I got an F. I got an A in gym, a B− in audiovisual, and everything else C's and D's. The asshole math teacher said I'd pass if I'd finish my work—Glen will love this. And Troy probably got all A's. I know what he'll say. "Shit, the army won't take you with these grades—dumb spooks do better. Maybe you could go live with your dumb uncle, Roy. He washes dishes in prison in Florida."

Another:

Went over to Craig's place. Stayed all night. Didn't call. Couldn't. Don't want to see mom. Why can't she leave him? He treats her like shit too. Last night he screamed at her plenty because she got between him and me. Craig says I can stay. His mom's not so sure, but his dad's an okay guy; he's an electrician, got his own business. Says he'd hire me anytime; I'm good with my hands; I gotta do something. Forget college, college will be a pain, who am I kidding? I can't get through college. I can't do any more learning!

The last page was filled with drawings, intricately detailed, their convoluted designs shaded expertly so they appeared interconnected. I painstakingly searched for any message, any recognizable clue that would jump out at me—what was he thinking at that moment? Was I reading too much into these pictures? And then I saw it—the barrel of a gun at the center of each design. The patterns always included the barrels of a rifle! I remember sensing goose bumps rising on the back of my neck. The next page was blank but for the following sentence:

> I thank my friends for always being there for me. Oh God, I couldn't have been here otherwise . . . and, and, my mom, Anna, too . . .

When we try to re-create the last few days of the life of a young person who has committed suicide, our goal is obviously directed to help the survivors. But for our work as healers, mentors, peers, and leaders to be effective, we need also to understand how to prevent suicide. As we develop profiles of suicidal adolescents, we focus on commonly known risk factors, whether internal or external. Access to the most lethal tools of destruction, like firearms, obviously increases the risk to someone truly intent on suicide.

Boys are much more successful in completing suicide than girls. In 55 percent of cases, boys use a gun.[1] Girls are generally less successful in killing themselves, whether because they have less access to guns, do not know how to use them, or prefer to use less painful methods (drugs, alcohol, carbon monoxide) is not entirely clear. Of the girls who successfully committed suicide in 1991, a higher percentage used firearms than in previous years. There is increasing evidence to indicate that those who do not have access to a gun are not as likely to kill themselves. Tim's notes, while full of references to his damaging relationship with his father and, as a result, his poor self-esteem, did not include any references to suicidal intentions. That choice came as a result of a particularly fierce fight with his father the day of the suicide. It was an impulsive decision, which might have been thwarted had no gun been available to him.

At our next session, Anna talked about her marriage to Glen, her years of unhappiness, and her inability to break away. In her mind, it was only Tim's death that finally enabled her to leave. Anna had recently moved to a room in a friend's house, and was looking for work. She had sought some help for her asthma, and was not constantly in respiratory distress. The extreme anguish of our first meeting remained, but she was able to speak more reflectively. I asked her about Tim's learning problems, sharing with her my observation that it was apparent from reading Tim's notebook that he had some severe learning disabilities. She seemed surprised, and then relieved. "I always knew he wasn't dumb, or lazy, like Glen said. Tim was never a good student, even when he was little. He used to go to a special class for reading and math help, and in junior high he almost didn't pass. In high school, the counselors told me that he should get some special testing, but our insurance didn't cover it, and Glen wouldn't pay the money for the tests. It's real expensive."

It wasn't a startling revelation. Testing is terribly costly, anywhere from $800 to $1,200 depending on the range of tests and who is administering them. Interpreting the results and providing remediation can also be expensive. Although all schools are mandated by law to provide special educational services to those children who need them, parents are not always aware of their rights in this regard. Services are not universally available in all school districts.

Certain learning disabilities are considered risk factors not only for depression and suicide but also for antisocial behaviors (juvenile delinquency, crime). I explained these linkages to Anna. I hoped that as Anna came to understand that there were clear markers contributing to Tim's suicide, such as impulsivity (common among children with learning disabilities) and school failure, as well as the emotional abuse, she would begin her own healing process. Perhaps she could forgive herself for her lack of resolve.

Neither Glen nor Troy would agree to come to a meeting. Glen didn't return our calls, and Troy, after promising twice to show up, told his mother he was not comfortable talking to a therapist. Their lack of cooperation made it more imperative for Anna to find some resolution, both around Tim's death and also around her decision to leave Glen.

I made some gentle attempts at helping Anna talk about the day of Tim's suicide; however, it wasn't until our last session that she herself brought it up.

"It was a Thursday, and Tim and Glen had not talked for days. I knew Glen was looking for a fight; he had been bugging Tim all week and Tim would just walk away in the middle. He wouldn't even let Glen finish talking. That made Glen even meaner. Tim was late because of basketball practice and while he was gone the school counselor called and left a message. Glen asked the counselor what it was about, but he wouldn't say. When Tim walked in, Glen right away got on him about the counselor. He was really carrying on, and all of a sudden, Tim grabbed him, grabbed both of Glen's arms, and shook him real hard. Glen had big bruises on his arms for days afterwards." Anna snorted loudly, happily, unashamedly, at the recollection. "Tim was in his face, nose to nose—screaming, yelling, that he was going for counseling because of how horrible his dad treated him; he said for the last year he had made sure every teacher in the school knew Glen was a rotten, stinking bastard. That's what he called his dad." Anna fished through her bag in search of something—her inhaler, it turned out. She inhaled and took a deep breath.

"You know, the craziest thing is, right then, I thought Glen was going to die. I thought he'd have a heart attack right there. He's got high blood pressure, he's not in such great shape anymore; he turned purple, he got his hand away and slapped Tim, hard across his face. Tim ran off, and as he was leaving the kitchen, he punched his fist right through the wall. Tim was always such a peaceful kid, I couldn't believe it. You know, I was glad for what Tim said to him—there it was, all out there. I wish I had said it, believe me, I wish I had."

Anna's voice was fading, but she continued, one hand clutching her inhaler, the other a wad of tissues. "We heard the door slam, and then Troy came running into the kitchen—'Dad, quick—your gun! Tim's out back. He's got your gun!' They thought Tim was going to kill Glen. They got to the back door, looked out the window. Troy told me later, Tim stared right at them, stuck the gun in his mouth, and fired. I passed out. I couldn't breathe at all; when the ambulance came, they had to give me oxygen. There was nothing they could do for Tim."

"You had no idea Tim was thinking about suicide?"

"Never. I talked to his school counselors. They said when they met with him the last time he only wanted to talk about leaving things behind, leaving home. He was the best athlete, sports were going to be his scholarship, his way out of Glen's life. Out of my life. God, I wish I could have made it better for him."

In situations of abuse, when one parent/adult is the primary abuser, questions are often raised about complicity by the other parent/adult. Why didn't the spouse intervene in some assertive way to stop the abuse? How can a parent knowingly stand by and watch his or her child's self-esteem be constantly undermined—or worse?

Her own feelings of inadequacy kept Anna in a marriage that was as emotionally abusive for her as it was for Tim. She had long ago given up on changing Glen; instead, she had concentrated on passively protecting Tim and "looking after the boys," much as she had looked after her father when her mother had died. While she couldn't save Tim, now, by leaving her marriage, Anna was attempting to acknowledge to herself that she had failed Tim. That was her real struggle—her feeling that she had contributed to his ongoing unhappiness and, in some way, to his death.

The literature on abuse is not always kind to persons like Anna—weak, passive bystanders in a cycle of abuse and pain. Some would argue that they are not victims, but accomplices, and deserve the same vilification as the abuser.

Is that a judgment that I could make of Anna? The issues in her life were more complex. When I terminated our meetings, I was satisfied that Anna had found some answers about Tim's suicide. She had found a job as a salesclerk in a card shop, and continued to live at her friend's place rent-free in exchange for some part-time baby-sitting. I referred her for therapy to a social worker whose office was not far from her work. Months later, I found out that she had only come to the first two sessions. At Christmas I received a card and note from Anna. It reads as follows:

> Dear Dr. Slaby:
> Just a note to say thank you again for all your help. I'm feeling much better, even though every day I think of Tim. I hope you won't be disappointed, but I moved back with Glen. It's hard sometimes, but I can't stand being alone and I don't want to lose Troy too. Sometimes, there are no choices. Take care, and thank you.

It's rarely possible to enforce choices for others, whether we are parents, educators, or health-care providers. Hopefully, counseling can help people to better understand their own choices and give them the inner strength to make ones that are the least harmful. Tragically, Tim had impulsively made his choice a fatal one. Anna had made her choice also.

■ ■ ■

The outcome of my work with Anna Morgan was disappointing. I had hoped that her choices would bring her some peace of mind. Her decision to return to Glen merely represented the least anxiety-provoking solution. She did not resolve the relationship between her husband's abuse of Tim and her own need to be passive. Her passivity maintained her in her role of abused wife and mother.

I have heard several stories like Tim's in my study. Being victimized within the family and then subsequently not caring enough to live is very common among adolescents who choose suicide. Paradoxically, the child who is abused may seek revictimization, a repetition of the painful abuse heaped on him or her by the parent. Revictimization can take on many forms—for example, unprotected sex, drug experimentation, criminal activity, and disregard for school or work. Intentional self-harm is another way that teens add to the abuse already experienced. Glen's emotional abuse of Tim robbed him of his desire and ability to value himself and to stand up to life's adversity.

In a perverse way, abuse can teach young people that they can survive the most horrible situations and go on, even while it makes them vulnerable to completely crushing and intolerable feelings. Their resilience can be destroyed by seemingly trivial life events. Tim—the joker, the athlete—had survived much. The day he died might have been one more day of survivable verbal and emotional abuse. But that day he was particularly vulnerable to his own pain, anger, and impulsivity. The gun was there and he would not survive.

Seven

SAVED BY GOD

I can't take the pain any more; it doesn't get better, only worse. To my mom and dad—don't feel bad—your life will be better with me gone—this is my decision, no matter what you think, I'm doing this for me.

To my friends—thanks, it was great—we had some great times, too bad there weren't enough of them.

To my coach—don't feel bad—I would have done this even if I made the team . . . it didn't matter any more . . . nothing does; nobody knows how much pain I'm in. I want the pain to end! Life has failed me as much as I have failed it.

Bret Groh, two months short of his fifteenth birthday, wrote this note a week before he twisted an old clothesline into a noose and tried to hang himself from a beam in the ceiling of the family room of his house. His parents had gone to a meeting at their church, and his younger brother and sister were at sports activities. By chance, his father, Mark, arrived minutes later to pick up something he had left at home. As he drove into the back driveway, he could see his son dangling in the window. He raced in and cut him down. Bret was semiconscious but alive. In the ambulance, his father held onto his son's hand and recited prayers and psalms for his recovery. His wife, Barbara, joined him at the hospital an hour later.

Teens who have been depressed and have made and/or completed suicide attempts have many behaviors in common. Somewhere in their despondency, in their lonely and ultimately elusive search for answers, the options they perceive to achieve happiness become narrow, limited. The fact that suicide is even considered a credible option is an obvious sign, often coming too late, of just how few options they actually perceive.

Many "typical" symptoms of depression—a radical change in behavior and in activities, sleeping all the time, irritability, a lack of appetite—may occur in some form; however, these signs may be recognized only with 20/20 hindsight. Adolescence may be a stormy time, and too often depressive symptoms may be misread as teenage turmoil.

Bret remained in the hospital for four days, and during that time his parents were referred to the depression clinic by both the emergency room physician and the minister of their fundamentalist church.

The resident who saw Bret after his suicide attempt had written routine notes in his chart:

Fourteen-year-old boy, brought in by ambulance, accompanied by father, and joined by mother shortly afterwards. Teen on oxygen at admission, semiconscious; on examination, there were no signs of injury on his body with the exception of large fresh welts around his neck, and a scar from an earlier appendectomy.

Parents are both very distraught, stating that Bret has no history of depression, no previous suicide attempts, drug or alcohol use. Blood and urine samples confirm no recent drug use. Neurological testing shows no brain damage. Upon waking, patient was well oriented in all three spheres, noncommunicative, monosyllabic, and, much later, angry at having to remain in the hospital. Parents are confused, frightened, but not very psychologically aware. Bret refuses to speak with me or any other staff member. I am recommending immediate psychiatric assessment and evaluation in the Depression Clinic. For the moment and until assessment, I have prescribed Xanax to ease his anxiety and worry for the next two days. Parents are unhappy at the prospect of their son taking any drugs, and I have reassured them that it is only temporary. I reviewed side effects and the potential for dependency developing with them.

They seem very suspicious of anything to do with psychiatry. They have made this very clear to me.

Bret's story is included in this book for a number of reasons. The first is that he was saved, and was shaken by the enormity of his close call with death and grateful for his rescue. His was not a "risk and rescue" gesture; he fully expected to die. Second, Bret and his family were deeply religious, and the strength of their religious faith had both positive and negative consequences for his recovery and future well-being. The final reason was that Bret typified features of depressed young boys and their families whom I see in therapy and in consultation. Bret and his family kept me at arm's length. My interactions with them were polite and superficial, so that the goal changed from trying to find out what precipitated the suicide attempt to keeping them in touch with me until I felt Bret was safe.

Despite a heightened awareness of the role of psychology in medicine and, more recently, the role of biology in psychiatry, many young people and their families are very reluctant to enter into the therapeutic process. For them, the mind represents the last bastion of privacy, personal choice, and dignity. Any examination of this inner territory is so threatening that barriers are immediately erected and preserved.

When I met with Mark and Barbara Groh the second day of Bret's hospital stay, they were still reeling from the shock of how close they had come to losing their oldest son. Nevertheless, they were not pleased at having to see a psychiatrist. At their insistence, Bret was not involved in the initial meeting. I had no difficulty with this provision, because I understood that they needed to check me out, to make sure I wasn't going to remove their control over their son's care or suggest some far-out rationale for Bret's suicide attempt.

They were both waiting in the small anteroom on the adolescent psychiatry floor. Mark, short and stocky, projected an assertive, defiant attitude as we made our introductions, letting me know immediately that this meeting was a waste of time. Barbara, by contrast, seemed nervous and unsure about what was happening. She didn't speak at all during the entire hour we spent together, but held onto her husband's arm with one hand, her other hand resting on top of a Bible. She concentrated on watching her husband's responses, as if by reading his lips she could gain some insight into what had happened to her son.

"You must feel so fortunate today," I began, "I understand that you saved Bret's life."

Mark responded, "It wasn't me, it was God, Dr. Slaby. I never forget anything, and that night I left a budget report for my meeting at home. It was meant to be. But you're right on one thing. I am very grateful. We both are."

"I will be speaking to Bret in the next few days, but in the meantime maybe you can help me understand what might have made Bret try to kill himself."

Mark shook his head: "I don't believe in psychology. I think you people take kids away from the church, from their parents; it's all in there, it's all in the Bible. If people spent more time thinking about what the Bible teaches us, this world wouldn't be in such a mess. Reverend Morrisey and Dr. Fielding both said we had to come and meet with you. Dr. Fielding said we should talk about Bret and us, and the reverend told us that you are doing some kind of research for a book about kids and suicide. I just don't think we can help you. We work hard, all of us, we love our children, we guide them, we go to church. You won't find anything crazy in our family, I can tell you that."

"Well, let's start with Bret. Did you notice anything different about him in the last few months? Was he sad? Did he seem to be acting unusual?"

Mark shook his head. "Bret is the best son anyone could have. He's never been in any trouble. Teachers like him; everyone does. I don't know what this is about."

It was a slow, difficult hour. All the standard questions about family life, Bret's activities, medical history, school performance, and friendships elicited terse "answers." Family life was "normal," no conflicts; Bret was a C student in a prevocational program in junior high school. He was very active and successful in sports, lettered in wrestling and hockey, and played racquetball twice a week. He was involved in church activities, worked with other kids in Sunday school programs, church bowling league, and religious retreats.

I told the Grohs about my work with depressed teens and described the research. I tried to reassure Mark and Barbara, telling them that I wanted to be sure that Bret would get the most effective medical attention; I wanted to understand why he had made this serious attempt. Most important, I added, I hoped through the research to prevent future suicide attempts in other teens, and perhaps in their son as well.

Neither parent seemed moved by this information, not at all. I attributed it to the shock that they were feeling. However, although they were shaken, it was obvious that their suspicions about psychiatry were unshakable. In Mark Groh's eyes, our meeting was a formality, part of the nuisance bureaucracy that comes with a crisis. He was caring and concerned about his son, but he remained distant from the mental health approach and removed from the process of intervention that was offered.

We met again prior to Bret's discharge from the hospital, but without Bret, who refused to be an active participant. Mark said that while his son was deeply ashamed about his attempt he was definitely not depressed. At the time of discharge, Bret was not taking any medication and did not, in Mark's opinion, seem to need it. The psychiatric resident in charge of his case attended the meeting and agreed that Bret did not appear to be depressed.

Before the meeting ended, I insisted, "I would like Bret to be here, while we discuss some follow-up plans."

Reluctantly, Mark went to retrieve Bret from the patient lounge, where he was waiting while his discharge was being processed.

Bret wore many of the typical high school status symbols—a letter jacket, stud in his left ear, carefully sculpted hair, and the requisite faded jeans. He appeared as "cool" as any teen you might see at the local mall. He was quite short for a boy his age, not much taller than five feet two inches, but very muscular. I could well imagine that his height might trouble him despite his build. I was able to schedule a follow-up appointment four days after his discharge. Surprisingly, Bret did not express any of the resistance to speaking with me that I had anticipated.

Barbara came with Bret to the first meeting. She looked like she hadn't slept in days. The dark circles under her eyes were a grim reminder of the chaos she had lived through only days earlier. As she sat down on the sofa, she began to crack her knuckles nervously. Bret started to sit down near his mother, looked around, and instead chose a straight-back chair near the door. I asked him to move it closer, and he grudgingly slid over.

I began, "Bret, Dr. Fielding, the doctor in the emergency room, called me yesterday. He said he couldn't be here but really emphasized the need to hold this meeting. He told me your father saved you from suicide. You're very lucky. I'm glad you're here to talk about it."

Bret shifted in his seat, his head bowed, speaking in a muf-fled, bored drawl. I had trouble hearing him, so I moved closer.

"My dad said to say he can't come today because he can't take off any more time from work. He said to tell you he's been docked for two days already. Listen, my dad's right. I wasn't meant to die last week, that's all. There's no more to tell. I don't need to be here."

Barbara watched Bret silently. I looked at her, hoping she could contribute something, some phrase, perhaps an event that might engage Bret so that he could begin to think about his issues and feelings. But she continued to look at me vacantly, unaware that her only response was the incessant crack of her knuckles.

I gently questioned Bret, "I want to understand what led you to try hanging yourself when everything in your life was going so well."

"It wasn't."

"You mean you faced things that bothered you?"

"I guess," he shrugged.

"You say things weren't going well in your life. Like what?"

Bret shifted in his seat. "I got kicked off the hockey team."

"Why?"

"I don't know."

"You weren't playing as well as before?"

"No! That's not why!"

Bret looked around the room, silent, defiant at the suggestion that his game had slipped.

Such reluctance to speak is very common with teenage boys. Most therapists find sessions with them frustrating because it is so difficult to elicit a response. One way to approach these boys is to begin with the larger picture—in Bret's case, things were not going well—and then, move from there to specifics. What happened on the hockey team? And then, were things falling apart in a class? What about friends? Slowly, the circles become smaller and smaller, so the issues become more and more distinct. When parents are open to psychological intervention these efforts are infinitely easier, even though parents, for many reasons, may not be effective in asking such questions. Sometimes they are consumed by anger at the child or at each other, they themselves may be depressed or they have some instinctive awareness and guilt that they have contributed to their child's desperation and feel overwhelmingly guilty about that. In Bret's case, his parents were simply unable to feel secure or positive about psychology. Either Barbara or Mark joined me in each of the meetings with Bret, more to monitor me, to protect Bret, than to contribute. Theirs was never a hostile presence, and they never interfered; they were just there. Their difficulty with the therapeutic process, their inability to think in psychological terms, was as relevant to our work as their total involvement would have been.

I asked Bret what happened with the hockey team. He responded, "I got kicked off because I missed practice and I mouthed off to the coach."

Bret had always been a team leader—not only a good athlete but also a good sport—so when he began to play rough, get more penalties, and act inappropriately aggressive even with teammates, his coach became concerned. He had made a visit to the guidance counselor a condition of staying on the team. I asked Bret about those meetings.

"I only went to one meeting; I skipped the others. I didn't like talking to her. She was nice and everything; it wasn't that. I don't know, I don't talk well to girls."

"You mean girls your own age?"

"All girls, any girls."

"So things on the team didn't change?"

"Nope."

"What did the coach say when he kicked you off?"

"I was a sore loser, argued with everyone, wasn't at practice. He had a list, like I was a juvenile delinquent or something. I got the last laugh though. After I left the team they lost three of their next four games. What a jerk!"

Later, I went back to the topic of girls, "You said you don't talk well to girls. Does that mean you think girls don't like you?"

More shrugs. "I never heard them say they don't like me. But they still don't talk to me."

"Do you think you're shy?"

"Maybe."

"Do you have any other idea why girls don't talk to you?"

He nodded, " 'Cause I'm short. I'm the shortest in the class. Most of the girls are taller than me."

This was what I wanted to stumble onto during our conversation. It's the kind of answer that comes up only once and is not emphasized by the teen. It is the wedge—a small clue into what is troubling this emerging, sweet-faced teen.

Bret began to talk about feeling different since beginning junior high. Initially, the main focus was his height. While his classmates were beginning major growth spurts, he remained short. His height became the first of many perceived deficiencies that he obsessed about. He was awkward around girls—proof to him of how inept and unattractive he was.

As his self-esteem plummeted and his depression progressed, his behavior in all his activities changed. Since athletics were so important to him, the changes were most apparent in hockey and wrestling. He was kicked off the hockey team and he was booed at wrestling tournaments because he was so aggressive. He became more irritable, blaming others for his mistakes.

Church became the only place where he did not regress. He rarely allowed his argumentative side to be seen by his father, whom he seemed to hold in awe. He focused on his "mistakes, screw-ups," gradually isolated himself from his old friends and activities, preferring instead to either remain in his room and obsess about his failures or hang out with a crowd known to "live fast and loose."

"I was like one of the 'dirtballs' at school."

"How did your parents react?"

"They didn't know."

"Did you feel happier hanging around these kids?"

Bret shook his head: "The same. I didn't care much who I was with, all I could think about was—if things don't get better soon, I don't know what I'm going to do. If I lose my hockey game, if I'm not on the wrestling team, if I don't pass my math test . . . if I don't do this or that—and I didn't do any of it. I was so out of it I ran in front of a car. But the guy driving must have had nerves of steel. He slammed on his brakes and missed me. It was weird—like, I could have been killed then, but I wasn't."

"Did you run in front of the car on purpose?"

"No way, but that's when I figured out how easy it would be to kill myself."

"Did you take any drugs when you were with those kids?"

"No, but they thought I did; the guys who took drugs were worse off than me. They had money and stuff, but they were wired—buzzed out all the time. Some of them, even their parents took drugs. How could I feel better? I didn't fit in anywhere."

Bret returned to school the day after he left the hospital. It was an awkward transition. He didn't know what to say to his friends and teammates about his stay in the hospital. At the end of his first week at school we held our next meeting. Both parents attended this session. We talked about what his experience had taught him and what he could say when friends asked about it.

"I know what I did was dumb. I'll never try anything like that again, that's for sure. I don't even know why. So why would I want to talk about it? Everyone will think I'm weird."

I persisted, "Well, let's talk about it here. What made you think that killing yourself was the answer?"

Bret looked at his father, sitting across from him. He paused a moment and then answered, "Lots of things. Getting kicked off the hockey team was the worst. It wasn't fair, that's all, and I knew there was no way the coach would let me back on. The guys on the team were ignoring me, girls never look at me anyways because, you know, I told you, I'm short. My mom and dad were mad at me, told me I was a disappointment to them. They didn't need to say anything, I knew what they were thinking. They like things always to be the same."

Mark was troubled with Bret's explanation: "You know that's not the way it was. Sure I was mad. You were hanging around with those bums. They have no rules at home, no church, just drinking and drugs. You got an earring—I hate that earring. No, I wasn't going to let my kid turn out like those jerks. Mouthing off to me—you never did that before. And you were getting into trouble on the team. I had good reason to be mad."

Now Bret was challenging his dad. "And my mom—all she did was get on my case, criticized me all the time. I always felt like a two-year-old at home. If it wasn't her way, it was the highway, she would say! My mom, she taught me how to hate."

It was hard for me to imagine Barbara exhibiting any kind of strong emotions, let alone anything angry enough to elicit hate. That she could teach Bret to hate, to try to end his life—it just didn't fit.

I asked, "What was your mother getting on your case about?"

"Mainly school, church, everything. Do I have to answer all these questions? I'm telling you, I'll never do it again, okay, I promise!" Bret slumped back in his seat, fidgeting with the letter on his jacket sleeve.

"Sit up straight, and show some respect."

Mark's command to his son was absolute, unequivocal. Bret sat up, rolled his eyes at me, and, with one eye on his father, muttered, "Sorry."

"Were you having trouble in school?" I asked.

He nodded, "I really had dumb teachers this year, that's why. I never did so bad before. At first, I tried, I really did."

Teens who become debilitated by depression usually exhibit something we call a "mutual affective state." This means that their actions mirror their feelings about themselves: "If I feel bad about myself, I'm going to give others reasons to feel bad about me." Bret became mired in this cycle very early into his depression. His ruminations about his height escalated and the behaviors that were meant to compensate for his size became more aggressive, so that he was rejected in every sphere he tackled— sports, schoolwork, friendships, family relationships. With each new rejection, his view of himself as a "loser" was reinforced.

"Did you plan your suicide for a long time?"

"No. Everyone left the house, and I was just sitting there. I was thinking about my report card, and what my dad would say when he saw it. I was tired of feeling like I couldn't do anything right, and I knew nothing was going to change, I could tell. So, the idea just crossed my mind."

"Your dad cut you down pretty quickly, Bret. Do you remember feeling anything? Were you aware of anything when you were still hanging there?"

"I was very scared when I knocked down the chair. I kept thinking, It's over, I don't have to worry anymore."

"Why do you think you were saved? Have you thought about that?"

"Oh, I know why. It was God. He sent my dad home to cut me down."

Mark started to say something to his son, stopped short, and then went on, addressing his remarks to us: "Look, I don't think we're getting anywhere talking about what happened anymore. We've done that. I don't want this to go on for weeks. Bret was foolish, and he's learned his lesson. He's promised me he's not going to hang around those kids anymore, and he's going to meet with his coach, see if he can get back on the team again. He's signed up for a Bible study group. Soon things will be back to normal."

It was obvious to me that I had the potential for only one more session with Bret, no more than that. It would be futile to pursue any other professional contact with Mark or Barbara regarding Bret's depressive episode. But before we would terminate our meetings, I needed some assurance that Bret was safe, that he and his parents would recognize the warning signs if they occurred again. I explained that it would be helpful to see Bret one more time, further along in his recovery. Given the serious nature of his suicide attempt, I explained, I would feel more secure if I could confirm that Bret was continuing to make good progress. Mark agreed to a final meeting at the end of the month. I requested that Barbara attend as well.

At our final meeting, Mark and Barbara appeared to be in better spirits than before. For them, time and faith were healing, and it showed on their faces. They were less anxious about talking to me, too, probably because they knew they didn't need to go through this again. Bret had put on some weight and was attending team practices in the hope that he'd be allowed back. He had a tutor in math and English and was trying very hard to catch up on his work and improve his grades. He seemed more at peace with himself, less sullen and withdrawn. This was who he was. He would never be outgoing or emotive, I thought. However, I needed to know that if he was feeling depressed again he would recognize it.

I asked, "How have things been going the last few weeks?"

"Okay, I guess. Better."

"How's school?"

"I'm busy again with sports, and I'm trying to get my grades up."

"Good. Have you felt sad again, at all?"

"No."

"Would you know it if you were beginning to feel miserable?"

"I think so."

"What would you do if that happened?"

"I guess I would, um, I would tell my dad I wasn't doing good."

"Do you think you could also call me if that happened?"

He lowered his eyes. "Maybe."

"Please understand that if you feel yourself, or your thoughts, coming down on yourself, angry, ticked off, you can call me at any time—at home or work. I'll want to talk to you."

Half of major depressions in young people go away without any treatment whatsoever, often to never reappear. I was counting on that happening for Bret. I asked him if I could have a few moments alone with his parents; he quickly left and took a seat in the waiting room.

"I wanted to know if you have any questions about Bret or about what to do if he becomes depressed again."

Mark answered: "Thank you. You've been very patient. And I think now you might have some information you can use in your book. But we're really doing fine now. You know, unlike a lot of people that you must see, we have our faith, our church, and that gives us all strength, more than psychology could ever.

"When I say this I'm not being critical, but it was clear to my wife and me from the beginning that we would not buy into any psychology of why Bret tried to kill himself. That's just the way we are. We find strength in our religion. We understand something about Bret's depression, and how it took over his day-to-day behavior, changed who he was. But we're his parents, and we know what's best for him. We learned a lot from this too, like we have to watch him more, make sure he never gets so caught up in himself again. We have to be more strict about who his friends are. There's lots of good kids at our church. And he has to be busy all the time. You can't get into mischief if you're too busy, now, can you?"

Mark got up and extended his hand. "This has been interesting—not easy, but interesting. Maybe you can come up and talk about your ideas to our youth group at our church someday. In the meantime, I've got to get back to work—gotta pay these medical bills, you know. Bret's going to be fine. He's a good boy, just needed some direction."

Mark and Barbara were very tightly defended against any psychological interpretation or intervention. Psychological explanations were simply too threatening, possibly too closely associated with few controls, unchristian liberal behavior; I would never know. They were very lucky once. I hoped that fate would not be tempted a second time.

■ ■ ■

Bret and his family taught me that each person saved from suicide understands his or her redemption uniquely. Bret and his family thought of his rescue entirely in religious terms. God intervened and saved his life by having his dad forget something, return home, and discover his son hanging from a beam in the family room. This was entirely understood as divine intervention, because dad almost never forgot things and the timing was such that Bret did not experience any permanent brain damage. Bret promised that because God saved him he would not go against His wishes and consider suicide in the future. His religious beliefs and understanding of his situation would have a permanent preventive effect.

I was also struck by the different defenses that Mark and Barbara used to come to terms with their son's depression and suicide attempt. It was very important for me not to judge and be critical of defenses that function outside of the realm of standard psychological explanations. The family's coping style was based on religion, rigid goals, and a lack of introspection. In fact, this family showed me that recovery is possible without a complete or deep understanding of the factors that contribute to depression. The down side to this family coping style was that it led to conflict between the depressed Bret and the family's rigid behavioral expectations. The parents, especially Barbara, were on Bret's case and critical of him rather than understanding the sadness that was driving his changed behaviors. Once they understood that depression was motivating this change in behavior, they were able to be more compassionate and less critical. The lessening of their criticism, in my opinion, definitely enhanced Bret's recovery.

When a teen attempts suicide we expect certain responses from the family, from medical and mental health professionals. One outgrowth of these response patterns is that the young person realizes that this attempt was serious behavior that has to be very carefully managed. Parents need to be informed and kept abreast of the treatment team's understanding of the youth's emotional and physical condition. In Bret's case, the parents never viewed the suicide attempt and its associated preexisting depression in the same way as the emergency room doctors and the treating professionals. I doubt that the parents could ever have achieved a similar or overlapping understanding of Bret's condition. What evolved, though, was that Mark and Barbara Groh respected this very different point of view, not necessarily ever understanding or accepting it. In addition, the treatment team came to value the family's coping style and reluctantly respected and supported it as effective for this family. This was one alternative way of handling a depressed and suicidal teen.

My overall goal in working with Bret was not treating depression, not providing clarification or insight or even a deeper understanding of the young person's problems. Rather, it was safety. I had to be satisfied that he would be safe adopting the previously used personal and family coping mechanisms. Safety can be ensured in a number of ways, including removing weapons, discarding unused medications, and providing frequent interactions among family members. Keeping busy with activities, peer involvement, and sports was part of Bret's safety net. Can I be absolutely sure that he will not again attempt suicide? Should I have insisted that Bret and his parents stay in treatment until they achieved insight? Obviously not. I am reasonably secure about his safety, based as it is on his family's stability and faith.

Eight

"COULD WE HAVE DONE MORE?"

> Dear Jessica:
> I know you probably don't understand why I did this. But I was very sick. Be a good girl and help mommy, daddy, Alan, and Josh get over the hard times. I expect you will be a very talented and happy Girl. I Love You.
> Love, Sarah

On the day Sarah wrote this note to Jessica, her sister, the world changed for the Cohen family, never to be the same again. On that day, Sarah Cohen turned on the ignition in her mother's car, closed the garage door, and cuddled her childhood teddy bear in the backseat until she fell into a permanent sleep. She was nineteen years old.

Once you have lost a loved one to suicide, can you ever stop feeling vulnerable? Can you ever stop asking where you failed? What you could have done differently? These were some of the questions that haunted Sarah's parents, Naomi and Larry Cohen, after her death. They first came to see me one year after her suicide, after hearing about our research through their grief support group.

The Cohens lived in a picturesque middle-class suburb in New England. Their move there was the last of three they had made since their marriage twenty-eight years before. Larry was a sales executive with a national clothing firm, and Naomi worked parttime as a librarian in a private school. Prior to their last move a year earlier, Sarah, the third of four children, had been an A student, a class leader. Then suddenly, without any warning, she seemed to change radically.

At my first meeting with Sarah's parents her father Larry explained: "It was all very sudden. She had finished two years of college; in fact, she had made the dean's list. She had a wonderful boyfriend, Peter, whom she'd known since her first day at college. Everything seemed to be going well. That summer she decided to take a job at a camp in the Berkshires so she could do something totally nonacademic. About two weeks after camp started we got these strange phone calls from her, really odd. We thought she was just having a hard time getting used to being with a bunch of spoiled twelve-year-olds. She had never been a camp counselor before and she didn't seem to like the campers at all. She said the other counselors weren't friendly, she couldn't do her job well. She wanted desperately to come home."

But it wasn't simply problems relating to adjustment. Looking back, the Cohens could see those first strange calls were symptomatic of an evolving illness. Larry continued: "She complained about hearing voices, she had horrible headaches, like migraines, only worse, because of these voices . . . and she seemed to be spending a lot of time alone in the bunk. Now I know it was crazy, but at the time we tried to convince her to stay at camp, not because we didn't want her at home, but because we couldn't understand why she was so miserable."

"Did you talk to any of the staff? Were they aware something was wrong?"

"Of course. They called us first because Sarah wasn't being responsible, and they were very critical of her. They told us she was uncooperative, she wasn't getting along with the staff or the campers. It was so unlike her that we decided there was no choice but to go and get her."

"What was she like when she got home? Did she seem depressed?"

"She looked worn out, completely different from before she left. But who knew about depression? Why would we? In the meantime, she was talking irrationally, really crazy, like 'I have worms in my brain'; or she would ask, 'What's wrong with my head?' or say, 'I'm very, very sick,' and 'People are talking too loud in my head.' Even then, our worst fear was that she had a brain tumor. She saw our internist, who examined her, did blood work, CAT scan, brain scan, everything. Finally the doctor told us that Sarah was profoundly depressed and had suicidal tendencies. We were stunned, but you know, we were so grateful because it wasn't cancer, it wasn't a tumor. We thought depression would be easy to beat compared to cancer!"

The internist who examined Sarah was unusual in her ability to identify both Sarah's depression and her suicidal potential. Nearly all studies show that most people who kill themselves are seen by their primary care physician three to six months before a suicide.[1] *Yet the possibility of depression or suicide is seldom raised.* Even in those instances where depression is clearly identified, patients may not get the help they need. Antidepressant medication is not recommended; or medicine with significant side effects is prescribed so that the patient stops taking it; or medicine may be given in inappropriate or inadequate dosages or not for a sufficient length of time. Sadly, while 60 percent of suicides result from depressive illness or other illnesses with depression, community surveys have shown that *less than one-third of all major depressions are ever treated.*[2]

Sarah's internist, however, was insistent. "The doctor warned us. She told us to take her behavior very, very seriously, and advised us to watch her closely because she was clearly suicidal. While Larry and I were still in her office, she called a psychologist in the clinic to see if she had time to see her the next day. We were shocked. We couldn't even imagine what this all meant."

Sarah met with the psychologist three times a week for intensive psychotherapy. Naomi shook her head as she spoke: "Who can say the end result would have been different . . . and don't get me wrong, I don't blame the doctor, but today, knowing what I do, I think she should have been hospitalized. It was all so strange, to see her crying all the time, weeping. She would say things like 'I don't belong,' 'I don't want to see anyone; I'm stupid,' or 'I'm so ugly, that's why I've never had friends.' "

Larry described the depression as becoming more severe daily. "I used to dread calling home. It was awful, because Sarah would get on the line and cry. I can't even express it, it was so horrible. Let me give you an example, something that happened that summer. We live on the water and one night, very late, Sarah comes into our room, wakes us, and says she's scared. Why? Because while she was out swimming she had actually thought about not swimming back. She never mentioned the word drown, but just that she wouldn't come back. For someone who said she was scared, she seemed really casual. Just lay there on the bed, looking up at the ceiling."

"What did you say to her when she shared that?"

Larry got up, shaking his fist in the direction of the heavens. "Nothing! Can you imagine—I said nothing! I just hugged her. I practically suffocated her, as if I could protect her . . . like when she was a little girl. I didn't know what to say. But I did call and tell her doctor the next morning."

At the end of the summer, Sarah remained agitated and depressed. She was adamant about not returning to college. But, after consulting with the psychologist, Larry and Naomi agreed it would be better if she returned to her classes, maybe taking two classes instead of four. Since school was only an hour away, she could continue her therapy and remain in close touch with her family. They reasoned that she would be more challenged among an academic community and with her friends. Very reluctantly, Sarah returned to school. "For three days we didn't hear from her at all. She never called. Apparently she stayed in her room, wouldn't see any of her friends, not even Peter."

Naomi Cohen described what happened next. "I went to pick her up on campus for her appointment with the psychologist. I had left a message on her answering machine that I would be there. She wasn't waiting at the door and no one knew where she was. I was frantic. I went to her room and found a note:

Dear Mom and Dad,

This is going to be the hardest letter for me to write but I must get it all out in the open. By now, you must realize that I've left school. I had to do it for a couple of reasons. First of all I was miserable here, I wasn't applying myself. Being that I left within two weeks, you will get back 90 percent of the tuition. I spent so much of your money lately and I don't want to waste any more. I also couldn't come home. Being at home and listening for the first time I realize how much of life I missed. Even though Josh and Jessica are at each other throats, I know it's normal. When I used to be mean to Jessica I would do it silently because I really had no reason for what I was doing. Also at home, I know I made it more tense. Everyone has their own problems and I have to do this one on my own. Right now I am not sure where I'm going or how I'm getting there. I have enough money to last for a while. I promise you I will either take a bus or a train to where I am going so don't worry about me. I got in touch with you so go about your everyday business and I promise I'll be okay. No matter what—I Love you.

Sarah

"I called her doctor immediately, and she reassured me, she wasn't concerned. Apparently they had talked in therapy about a trip to San Francisco some time in the future, when she was feeling better. Why San Francisco? Who knows? Later, after she died, I read it in her journal. She wrote that she had gone there to kill herself. The only thing that stopped her was that she decided to see Jessica, her sister."

Larry was home when Sarah called the next day. "She told me she was in San Francisco, and apologized for writing a bad check for her airline ticket. Now she badly wanted to see Jessica, in Florida, so I arranged for a ticket to be waiting for her at the airport. In our survivor group they told me that probably once she saw Jessica everything she needed to do was covered. I mean, she had actually thought this all out. I had no idea, none."

I asked, "How was her visit with Jessica?"

"Fine, they spent a long weekend together, hung out on the beach."

"Did Jessica get any sense of how depressed Sarah was?"

She told Jess that she'd been very depressed, not herself at all, but now her life was on track again. She seemed better for about a week when she got back, but then she became even more agitated, and there was no way she could be at school.

"She was up in the middle of the night—we could hear her wandering around. She ate very little, so she lost weight. She couldn't concentrate on anything—books, TV, not even on a dippy soap opera! She still talked about the pain in her head, how it was always there."

"Was she in therapy?"

"Oh yes, all along, she saw the therapist three times a wee';. Her therapist was very, uh, noncommittal when I would call to see how things were going. She was always warm to me, understanding that I was worried, but made it clear that, professionally, she couldn't share much with us."

Most parents, most people, are at a loss when their child or anyone close to them becomes mentally ill. They react with fear, with withdrawal at the bizarre behaviors and disinhibitions that they see in their loved ones. The Cohens had never before come face to face with psychiatric illness. They had no frame of reference; it was all simply overwhelming.

But when a crisis does occur, as it did with Sarah's profound symptoms, what is the best way for parents to respond? Sarah obviously had no inner resources still operative that could sustain her, so she became secretive, said odd things to her friends, her family. She exhibited many of the physical symptoms of depression, such as sleep disturbance, appetite changes, and crying spells. Collectively, these were all serious. How possible is it to make a judgment call during a crisis when you have no clue what would be best for your child? More and more uncomfortable, worried about Sarah's lack of progress, Larry and Naomi insisted on a meeting with the psychologist. She consented to a meeting on the condition that Sarah be a part of it. Although they came to the meeting together, at the last moment Sarah chose to wait outside.

Naomi described the sequence of events: "I have a brother who is a GP in another city. When things were rough I called him all the time for advice. He kept telling me I should ask about antidepressant medication. He insisted that I at least ask the psychologist if Sarah's depression was the kind that would respond to medication. Sarah had always been a 'purist'—a vegetarian, worried about the ozone layer, endangered animals, all of it. I knew that to her taking medicine was the same as putting dangerous chemicals in her body. I knew she simply would not do it. Basically, the psychologist said the same thing. Sarah would never take any pill, especially anything that might have side effects. What were we supposed to say? 'Never mind, we insist! Put her on medication anyhow'?"

The Cohens, like many parents I've spoken with in the same situation, were resigned to hoping that things would improve. And, like other parents in the midst of such pressure, they were unable to stand back and get some perspective. Admittedly, this is not an easy thing to do, but it is critically important to stand back and say, "This isn't working, we must try something else. Possibly a second opinion, or hospitalization." Somehow the danger signals were being accepted, minimized, and rationalized.

"The psychologist must have done something different after our meeting, because for the first time Sarah seemed to make some progress. She wasn't so tense; she could concentrate better. We were so relieved. We began to believe that therapy was finally working. There was no more talk about voices, brain disease. She was even able to take a job in a video store, joke around with us, read a novel. After five or six weeks like that her therapist cut her sessions down to twice a week. And then for a very short while it was once a week. It was a very short while because right after that she committed suicide."

Sarah's calm facade and her ability to manage with fewer therapy sessions were indications that she had come to a turning point. But it wasn't for the right reason. Suicidal patients are often very calm once they make the decision to kill themselves and formulate an absolute plan. Finally, they have a solution, a release from their pain. It's not that they want to die. If they could only recognize an alternative solution, they would.

Had the Cohens ever considered a second opinion? Naomi recalled that the psychologist had said early on that Sarah might be one of those cases that was resistant to help. "When we first met with her, after the first appointment, she was very straight with us. "Look, I don't know if I'm really going to be able to help Sarah; she's in bad shape. But I'll know very soon. If it's not working, I'll refer Sarah to someone else.' But she never did. At our second, our last meeting, we asked if she still thought she could help her. She said she had no doubt that Sarah had turned the corner."

I asked, "Did Sarah ever seem depressed to you when she was younger? Was there anything about her that was different?" Larry Cohen couldn't think of any obvious early warning signs of depression.

"Sarah was born three weeks prematurely, and weighed less than five pounds. Until she was almost a year we'd call her our fragile little bird, because she was so tiny, with those big eyes like a little chick. She did have a learning disability, but we never thought it was too serious. It was a reading handicap which was frustrating for her. Because she was very bright she always got into gifted programs in spite of it. She was the only child in the gifted program who had to take remedial reading at the same time. Except for reading, everything else was a breeze. Look at this picture"—Larry pulled a picture out of his wallet— "Do you see any unhappiness in that face?"

I wondered how many times Sarah's parents had looked through their photo albums to see if their memories of happiness, of joy were accurate? Had they ever sensed some vulnerability before, something they couldn't identify?

Larry continued, "When she was most frustrated in school,

even when she was little, she would say that she was a 'retard,' that she hated reading, was embarrassed to go to remediation classes." Later, in the midst of her depression, Sarah could recall only this hurt she felt because of her difficulty with reading; her feelings of being stupid and inadequate became foremost in her mind. Her depression distorted the magnitude of the learning disability, affected her schoolwork, and interfered with her ability to maintain friendships. This pattern was not unusual. Learning disabilities not only intensify feelings of frustration but may also increase the risks for depression.

The decision to commit suicide is always complex. But not everyone who is depressed or schizophrenic or manic-depressive commits suicide, even if he or she is never treated or is seemingly resistant to treatments. What are the factors that make the critical difference? One crucial component is the quality of distortions in thinking. People who are not perceiving the world accurately may act on confused data. If they are temporarily angry at someone, they must have nothing to do with them. If they see an opportunity for creative or business success, they may go for it without adequate planning. If they feel hopeless, they conclude that the feeling will never end and they consider suicide the best option. Life events are perceived differently when someone is depressed. In fact, when people are depressed, they selectively remember only negative life events. They even see neutral events negatively. For instance, a girl may be raised in a normal loving family, but when she is depressed she may see it as cold, depriving, and uncaring. After the depression is treated, she may once again remember her family as supportive and loving.

"What about her friends," I asked. "Did they notice any differences?"

"After Sarah died, her friends were devastated. She had written to each of them before she killed herself. She mailed the letters the day before she died. She told them each how much she cared about them. They told us that when they last saw her she seemed like a different person. She would just sit there in another world. They would say, 'Earth to Sarah. Earth to Sarah.'

They were kidding, but they were also trying to get some response. She didn't want to be with them, she made that very clear."

The Cohens were very grateful for the survivor movement. Both Larry and Naomi attributed any progress they'd made in dealing with Sarah's death to the information and support they'd received through the group Compassionate Friends. They, in turn, had made themselves available through religious organizations to other families who had someone die from suicide. In these meetings, they were very open about the circumstances of Sarah's death, sorrowful but not embarrassed or ashamed. Yet they had chosen not to tell Naomi's parents the circumstances of their granddaughter's death. Naomi explained, "My parents survived the Holocaust. They're in their eighties and live in Florida now. They have always looked at life negatively, and they definitely would have blamed me for Sarah's death. We didn't tell them the truth because of the stigma that still does exist, especially in their generation. They would have made some awful assumptions—she was on drugs, or pregnant, or probably that I wasn't a good mother. My mother has always been a very critical woman. I just couldn't have handled her questioning."

Many parents who the Cohens met in survivor groups were intensely angry that someone they loved without question died by suicide. Given the choice, they would have died themselves rather than lose their child.

The Cohens, though, were surprised at the anger families felt toward the person who committed suicide. Larry said, "It's so odd . . . most of the people in our survivor group were angry with the person who committed suicide. But we can't be angry at Sarah. She was the one who really suffered. We were never angry at her, even when she was so crazy, so sick. She's the one not here anymore. Our life goes on; it's never going to be what it was, but we're alive."

Their friends were loyal and supportive when they heard about Sarah's death. Many drove from other cities where the Cohens had lived earlier to be with them. Even when friends were uncomfortable or at a loss for words, the Cohens found their presence helpful.

Larry stressed, "The only thing worse than her dying was finding her body." The image of the discovery of the suicide forever remains in the mind of a survivor. Details are irrevocably etched into their souls. "Sarah was never the dramatic type. It never occurred to us that she might jump off a bridge like she thought about doing in San Francisco or that she might shoot herself. She killed herself with carbon monoxide, sitting in the back of our car reading a magazine. She left the motor running with her legs up on the seat, and the magazine and her teddy bear in her lap. When she was little she took that bear everyplace. We used to joke that we would frame it for her wedding gift. Except for the color of her skin, we might even have thought she was having a nap. For me, that memory is the worst, the one that still keeps me up at night."

It is almost impossible to imagine the horror of discovering a suicide. Generally the younger the person who finds the body, the more traumatic the long-term effect and the greater the danger of post-traumatic stress disorder. Post-traumatic stress disorder (PTSD) is characterized by intrusive memories of the discovery, recurrent nightmares, hypervigilance, and vague anxiety and depression. Sarah's eight-year-old brother, Josh, was there when his parents found the body, and he had symptoms of post-traumatic stress for years afterward.

Naomi described Josh's reaction: "When we got home that day, the day she killed herself, Josh was with us. When we found her, he ran out of the garage and locked himself in the bathroom. He stayed there until long after the ambulance left. I'm ashamed to admit that we were so hysterical that we didn't even go to him, comfort him. For a whole year he never mentioned Sarah by name, *never*."

Naomi tried to remember when they first took Josh to see a counselor. "I know it was much later, long after he should have had help, but he refused to see anyone for such a long time. By then he was having nightmares and terrible problems at school. When we left the house at night, no matter how late it was, he would be waiting by the window. It could be one o'clock in the morning and he would be sitting up there looking out. He did poorly in school, wouldn't get involved in sports, just stayed home with us. We tried to make it easier for Josh, but it took months and lots of behavioral problems at school before he got real help."

The loss of a sibling to suicide is a highly traumatic event. Most children and teens have an immature, fragile worldview, and obviously, most have no comprehension of the harsh realities of serious mental illness. Even more so than the surviving adults, they may obsess about what their contribution might have been to the suicide. If they were ever angry at their sibling (and all children are), they believe their anger may have caused him or her to die. After the suicide they can't undo the last fight, the angry words, or unspoken wishes. Their primary fear is that in some way they wished their sibling to die. In Josh's case, his fear was driven less by guilt and more by the fear of losing another family member. He has had classic symptoms of depression, anxiety, and post-traumatic stress disorder. For Josh, the legacy of Sarah's suicide has continued for five years, necessitating various periods of therapy.

Families struggling with how best to interact with a family member who is severely depressed or in crisis need to convey both support and direction in a positive manner. Ironically, that very positive attitude from family or friends may cause depressed persons to feel that no one really understands the depths of their hopelessness. They perceive that their very authentic and intense pain is being minimized. For family and friends, then, any affirming, positive response may become a lose-lose situation. Advice and guidance, therefore, must reflect an awareness of how incapacitating the depression is. Hopefully, the depressed teenager can incorporate the encouragement and direction and enhance his or her motivation and self-control.

The next time I met with the Cohens, their older son, Alan, was with them. Generally, my policy has been to invite family members to participate in meetings, but I never strong-arm anyone, no matter how convinced I am that it would help my work or them. Survivors have a right to privacy, and there is no advantage in compounding the pain or in appearing voyeuristic. Alan was interested in the book I was planning, and wanted the opportunity to share, to contribute by speaking about Sarah and about what helped and what interfered with his own healing.

A second-year law student, Alan stood six feet tall, with dark, wavy hair down to his shoulders. He was very relaxed and open, eager to meet with me. Naomi and Larry went out to have some coffee while we met. Alan was living at home at the time of the suicide and provided his own perspective. "The psychologist couldn't seem to get at the problem, maybe because everything was so sudden, so quick—Sarah went downhill right away. It had to be something medical, physical, not some psycho-junk. I mean, I studied psychology all through college. Sarah was in my textbook!" Alan's description of the illness was consistent with his parents' and with what we know about this type of episodic recurrent depression—healthy pre-suicide personality, with a clear drastic change in behavior occurring over a relatively short time.

Alan continued, "All of a sudden, Sarah was very, very unhappy. She left for camp in June—a month later she was all strange. I still don't know how she held it together at camp with the kids in her bunk. The last weekend, the one when she killed herself, she really worked on my parents to let her stay at home alone. She had seemed a lot better, so my parents gave in. It was the biggest mistake. In our support group, we learned that Sarah was typical. She knew we were going away for the weekend, and all along that's when she had planned to commit suicide."

I asked, "Do you think any one thing pushed her over the edge, or do you think she'd been depressed before?" Alan thought for a moment, and shook his head.

"She was away from her boyfriend, Peter, but they stayed in touch. He's a good guy; he was just totally loving to her all the time. When she was very depressed in the summer, though, she had some strange feelings about him too. She even wrote him a letter ending it, but she never mailed it. After she died, I found it in her dresser and tore it up. I'm convinced now that she would have killed herself no matter what. If it wasn't that weekend, it would have happened another time."

Alan also wanted to talk about finding her body, an experience that for some must be worked through again and again, even years later.

"My dad says he found Sarah, but really we all did. We had tried calling home a couple of times while we were on the road. No answer. On the way home everyone was quiet, unbelievably tense. Nobody said it, but we all were afraid of the same thing—we were going to find her dead when we got home. My father was speeding like crazy and he didn't talk at all. We drove our car into the garage. The other car was parked in the middle of the garage with the motor going. He jumped out; one by one, we followed. So we were all there with him but he physically found her. We knew . . . we knew before he opened the car door."

"What happened then? What did you do? Do you remember?"

Alan continued, "It was wild. It was really wild. I just screamed and Josh ran into the house. He was only eight. He didn't know what was really happening. My father was nuts—in kind of a blind frenzy. He called the paramedics. My mother threw up, right there in the garage. When the paramedics came they said there was nothing they could do. We had to make funeral arrangements and call all kinds of people—my sister, my uncle, our friends. I was totally numb. Everything was happening around me. I felt paralyzed—my feet felt like ice, like they feel when they fall asleep. My dad and I sat up that whole night together drinking scotch. I had never before seen him drink anything stronger than wine."

The numbness is characteristic of the survivor experience. "It can't be real." "Why did it happen to her?" "Dear God, please let us all awaken from this bad dream." "How can we go on?" There are no precedents. At some level, Alan had been prepared for this moment of discovery, "Even though I was hysterical, I realized that, somehow, I sort of prepared myself for finding her somewhere in the house when she didn't answer the phone. I knew that she would be dead when we got home. You know, if she had been killed in a car accident, there would have been no buildup at all, no anticipation. A sudden shock. Her suicide was different. I know it sounds like hindsight now, but the last two hours in the car, we knew it had to be bad. Besides, I had real clues, too."

"She had said something?"

Alan added, slowly, deliberately, "No, but I had found a suicide note in her room a long time ago. I never told anyone about it. I know now I made a terrible mistake. But I didn't know then. I probably helped Sarah kill herself by not saying anything, but I couldn't believe she was serious."

The suicide note was totally new information for me. "You didn't say anything to her either?"

Alan was almost pleading, now, whispering, "No. I couldn't, I didn't know what, how . . . I have it. I don't even know why I kept it." It was neatly folded in a pink envelope, with Sarah's name on the back:

> I am sorry tho, but live your lives to the fullest please. I can't ever explain myself. I don't know how to anymore. I am entirely gone. It's been hell for me. I don't like it and I can't tolerate myself anymore. Believe me, it is nobody's fault but my own.
> I'm scared but I am gone.

"Please don't you tell my parents. They would never say they blamed me, but I'd always know they did."

In that moment I had pressed the one button that Alan had never allowed anyone to touch before. Disregarding Sarah's suicide note was not unusual. Parents and friends have come in with suicide notes, sometimes two or three, written days, months, years before the actual event. At the time they found the note they needed to believe it was only a random thought, not a serious pledge. Only later did its ominous significance become clear. Alan had thought about this note, too. He had dreamed about it for almost two years.

He continued, "Sarah wrote that note before she'd been to San Francisco, before seeing Jessica. I must have convinced myself that the trip had been good for her, had cured her. I remember she talked nonstop the first night home, no crying at all."

"What do you remember most about her depression?"

"She couldn't do anything—read, watch TV, go for a walk. It's hard for me to think about those five months because I only want to remember the old Sarah. It's too awful any other way."

Alan was most worried about his brother, Josh. "When we'd go out, he'd phone at least three times to make sure we were okay. He didn't want to go to friends' houses, only have them come over to us. He's still different. I'd never say this to my parents, but I worry, maybe he's turning into Sarah. Is that possible?"

"I can understand why you'd worry about Josh. Remember that because of Sarah's depression and her suicide you are much more aware of the danger signals, more sensitive. I suspect you'll be watching Josh with a much more critical eye."

"That's true, I already am. But it's like what happens in the survivor group. When you talk about the suicide in a group like that, it's healthy. You listen to all these people who've gone through the exact same thing. You remember things, important signs we missed. We didn't always have to say it all. You could go around the room and read the same kind of story on all our faces. You know, I took a suicide prevention class after Sarah died. All twenty of us in the class were related to or knew someone who had killed themselves. I couldn't believe it."

Alan had brought Sarah's letters to read. Remembering her through her letters, her writings, helped him. The letters were witty descriptions of college life. She was active in campus groups and obviously enjoyed her studies. Her writing was labored, childlike, but she never mentioned her reading difficulties. She never talked about not being accepted. I could understand why this was how he preferred to remember her.

I met with Naomi and Larry Cohen several more times over the next six months. Certain routine events still evoked the same chilling memories. Coming home from a trip, for example, vividly recalled the situation when they found Sarah dead. Larry said, "It's very obvious to me. I'll always have the same feelings. I remember when we couldn't get her on the phone—I just knew something was wrong. When we walked into the house after finding her, a fifty dollar bill I had given her was on the kitchen table with all of her other money. There must have been two thousand dollars on the table. She had withdrawn all her money from the bank."

I met the Cohens for the last time late in November. The night before, at Larry's invitation, I had spoken to their suicide survivor meeting. He had been deeply moved by another family who had just lost a child to suicide without any immediate warning. "From the time we first were confronted with Sarah's depression to her first and only attempt, her suicide, was six months. Last night at our meeting you heard how those other parents talked. No previous warning. For a parent that's the toughest thing. How could their children ever reach that point of despair, and they as parents never recognize it? For us, a month earlier—in May—Sarah was fine. What do we do with that? I still haven't figured that out."

Part of what contributes to the delayed reaction to a traumatic event is the degree to which it is unanticipated, capricious. Perhaps parents and friends could have avoided it if they had seen it earlier, perhaps not. It is unpredictable. Studies have found that often the premorbid (before illness) functioning is normal. Can anyone of us become as sick as Sarah did that suddenly?

■　■　■

There are no simple models to inform families who experience a suicide of what to expect. No simple monolithic vision exists. Like the colorful chips in a kaleidoscope, they are always present but create a completely different picture for each viewer.

Anger is probably always present, but each family expresses and directs it differently. Larry and Naomi Cohen came to an understanding that given the many distortions of perception caused by depressive illness, for Sarah, their "fragile bird," suicide was the only way to stop the hurt permanently.

No one could rewrite Sarah's last six months. Would medication have prevented her swift deterioration, her suicide? Perhaps, but maybe not. *Some people cannot be saved.* Sometimes medication doesn't work, or it's the wrong medication, or they won't take medicine regularly, or at all. But in a crisis, it is critical not to become paralyzed or intimidated, either by the depression or by the professionals who give you an opinion. If symptoms persist, if there seems to be no improvement, ask why. Get the person into the hospital if necessary.

Studies using psychological scales that evaluate the dimensions of depression show that those individuals most likely to die by suicide are those who score high on the hopelessness scale.[3] It is critical to rebut that hopelessness—to be aggressive. When persons are acutely depressed, they can only relate to the dark side; their judgment is totally distorted. Those closest to them must direct them to the sunlight once again.

While struggling with the depressed teen over everyday behavioral issues, parents need to assess whether or not the youngster is getting better. How long should a parent wait before deciding that treatment is necessary or the treatment that the individual is currently receiving is not effective? If the course of treatment is stable, parents should be able to observe some incremental improvement over a three-to-four-month period. If the course continues to spiral downward and more severe symptoms are surfacing, it's important to get a different perspective quickly, definitely. Sarah's severe major depression should have been treated with both counseling and antidepressant medicine. Would the outcome have been any different if she had agreed to medication? Perhaps, but there is no guarantee. Nevertheless, the Cohens would have known that everything possible to treat the major depression was utilized.

In this instance, since Sarah's death her parents and siblings have struggled with the question of whether she would be alive today had she been provided with every modern method of treatment. Directing an older adolescent to treatment can be very difficult, especially, as in Sarah's case, when she is legally an adult. Because confidentiality between counselor and client is paramount, parents who press for additional or alternative treatments may be making their recommendations based on less than complete information. Parents must, above all else, keep their eye on the goal: namely, relief from the depression.

Sarah was resistant to medication. Most depressed people who are desperate will try medication if it is explained in a very direct, forthright manner. When the adolescent patient is not educated about the beneficial and therapeutic roles of antidepressant medicines, unrealistic expectations are placed on the other integral component of treatment, the counseling. Severe depression such as the one Sarah suffered should be viewed as requiring *both* counseling and medication.

There are some people who are resistant to modern treatments for depression. However, as new and more complex medicines are being developed, even these patients can be helped. When medication fails, hospitalization and other treatments for depression, namely electroconvulsive therapy (ECT), should be considered. Everything that can be done to save a life must be considered. Severe major depression should be considered as life-threatening as any other terminal medical condition. Immediate and consistent attention is a necessity.

"Guilt Kept Me Sane"

And why bother to live if one can't be useful?
You know, sometimes I really hate myself.
Once I even tried to take my life.
I thought death might be—well interesting.
But I realized finally that I was a good enough
person and decided to live.

In my effort to identify subjects for our research, I often wrote to members of the clergy in the community. In a letter I explained my mission to them: to better understand the causes of adolescent suicide and to help those who survive the loss of a young person to go on with their lives. About three months after he received the letter, Charles Monroe, the Curate of St. James Episcopal Church, called to tell me that the stepson of one of his trustees had died by suicide. The boy's mother, Mollie Bainbridge, was willing to speak to me. She had told him she would be relieved to talk to someone who could understand the agony she was experiencing.

She met with me over several months and told me with much pain and tenderness the story of the life and death of her extraordinary son. The cause of his death, she contended, was at least in part or perhaps even entirely her fault. Her explanations were revealed only with time and after much anguished soul-searching.

Mollie Bainbridge impressed me as an elegant and outgoing woman. She had the warm, comfortable sensuality that comes to some people with age. Mollie would always look good, perhaps even better with the years. In all our meetings, Mollie was struggling to know more. Often insight comes only with the struggle for adequate words, when a vocabulary that includes this horror can be found. I was struggling, as always, to understand. After expressing my condolences for her loss, I explained anew why we were meeting. Mollie then began by providing me with some facts about Kent's life and death.

"Kent was nineteen-years-old when he died, but he had not lived at home on a regular basis since he was fifteen. In fact, we were still married at the time Kent left home. He was always asocial and so uncontrollable as a teenager. He would not accept any authority or advice, not from anyone. Typical teenage things like curfews, not showing up at school, smoking, not being part of family activities, became the cause of unbelievable fights. Everything was extreme. At one point, we talked to our doctor, and he suggested that Kent be evaluated at Franklin Lodge [an exclusive private psychiatric hospital]. The doctors recommended that Kent live away from us, which I frankly couldn't understand, but we took their advice. So at fifteen, Kent got his own apartment. It wasn't until much later that he was diagnosed with schizophrenia."

She went on to describe her son in terms often used to describe teens who die by suicide. He was "different," "brighter," "more sensitive," and "more creative." Typically, suicides sometimes seem older than their years. They are considered precocious, unusual. "Kent was brilliant beyond belief. I really feel in my heart that a source of his problem was that he was never a child; he was always trying to relate on an adult level. Even at two he was not like the other kids. Somewhere along the line he skipped growing up like a normal kid. That's what I think."

I asked, "Was Kent very affected by the breakup of your marriage?"

"I guess I should explain, Dr. Slaby, that Kent's dad, Tom,

started to act very bizarre during the last three years of our marriage, almost at the same time Kent began adolescence. Kent had just begun to be really impossible. I just naturally put it together that his dad's craziness was the reason."

"Can you tell me what kind of craziness you mean?"

"Tom started to become suspicious of most people—his staff, clients, and friends. He stopped seeing friends; he just refused all invitations. I would go out, and he'd stay home, usually reading in bed with the remote to the TV. He refused to get help. I spoke to a psychiatrist, a neighbor of ours, and explained what was happening to Kent and to Tom. He suggested that if I told Tom I needed help, he might be willing to see someone to talk about me, and in that way he could be evaluated."

Under protest, eventually Tom accompanied Mollie to a psychiatrist who met with each of them separately. Mollie shared his findings: "He said that Tom was very likely a paranoid schizophrenic. This was mind-boggling to me, unbelievable, because for the first fifteen years of our marriage, despite his eccentricities, he always seemed able to cope with life. It was only in the last three years he began acting in stranger and stranger ways. You can't imagine what my life was like. Tom and Kent were each having problems I could barely deal with. I was in over my head but couldn't admit it."

"How did Kent react to his dad?"

Mollie continued: "Kent seemed to sense Tom's weakness. He would bully his dad when he was acting the most bizarre. They had terrible arguments. I thought that Kent had to be going through something temporary. It had to pass. I mean, he was a teenager, that's what teenagers do. Frankly, I couldn't even begin to understand, let alone accept, Tom's diagnosis. The doctor talked to both of us. He wanted to start Tom on medication, but I see now that neither of us was listening to him, not really. I tried to get help for Kent. When I look back now, I can see how impossible this was, how unrealistic it was for me to deny how sick they both were."

Mollie's self-recriminations and her pain were evident and typical of family members. The illnesses that lead to suicide are often found in various degrees in other family members, making getting help all the more difficult for the person best able to function—in this case, Mollie. A son may be using drugs and a parent may be an alcoholic. A daughter may have volatile mood swings similar to her mother. Sometimes the person is almost too close to the situation to recognize or accept the similarities. Tragically, when the crisis occurs, the troubled parent is often emotionally or physically absent—he or she may have abandoned the family, divorced, or for all intents and purposes become absent by virtue of the mood disturbance. It is impossible for this spouse to be supportive or helpful. An added complication is that major depressive illnesses may distort perception, clouding the person's awareness of the acute need for help and cooperation. This was so in Kent's case.

Kent refused any kind of help because he could always rely on his quick intelligence to talk his way out of things. It really masked his sickness, his craziness. Just before he turned sixteen, Kent's behavior became so unpredictable that his psychiatrist arranged for him to be admitted at Franklin Lodge again. He ran away after four days, immediately after hearing that his parents had separated.

Kent, who already appeared to be suffering strain both from his father's illness and erratic behavior and from his own emerging adolescence, was even more troubled by his parents' separation. Despite the history of bitter father-son conflicts, Tom, alone, suspicious, and frightened, sought support and comfort from Kent. However, Kent was unable to provide it.

As Mollie told it, "Kent became a crutch for his dad because Tom was alone. He got Kent to do errands so that he wouldn't have to leave the house. He used Kent to complain about me. Tom saw himself as the victim. Kent knew his father was manipulating him, but Tom was kind of . . . of pathetic. He had to have played on Kent's guilt about their fights when we were still together. But I wouldn't tolerate Kent's behavior when he was disruptive. Our lives had already been too dominated by his mood swings and his difficult temperament. I couldn't risk losing his sisters and brother too."

Mollie's face was pained as she recalled how torn she had felt at that time. A parent can never win points with a child by denigrating the other parent, no matter how strained the situation may be or how accurate the comments. Tom Bainbridge's cruel comments regarding Mollie troubled Kent, so much so that he realized that his dad had not changed very much, that he was still difficult. Kent was in a no-win situation. When he lived with his father, he would hear constant criticism of his mother, whom he alternately loved and hated. When he lived with his mother he had to comply by her rules, he had to conform to the larger household. He was starting to experience more radical changes in behavior, typical of his illness, diagnosed much later as schizophrenia and depression. It was becoming more impossible to live at home with younger siblings, who also demanded their mother's love and attention.

What appeared to be a dislike of both parents may really have been Kent acting out his rejection of dependency on his family. It was a difficult, confusing time for him. The changes that were occurring—the separation, his father's schizophrenia, his own changing behaviors—together they were overwhelming.

Mollie ended the session by sharing more about Kent's progress in high school despite his severe social and emotional problems. He took some summer courses at the same Ivy League university his father had attended and did as well as some graduate students in the same class. At the end of his sophomore year, he switched from his prep school an hour away from home to attend a public high school. At the time, his prep school counselor wrote a recommendation, describing Kent as a voracious reader, with a fantastic vocabulary, a highly sensitive young man with a wonderful sense of humor, a great raconteur, *but not a child.*"

The same frustration that Kent's mother felt in relating to his father for the past three years as he became progressively more disturbed, she now experienced with Kent. It was all too familiar, and it was painful. When Kent was home, he was ambivalent about being there. No sooner had he unpacked his bags than he acted out.

Mollie described her frustration: "I had a lot of love to give. I was always trying to hug him and kiss him, and he couldn't give anything back. It was frustrating for me. It was too close, too much like the problems I had with my husband. I think that Kent clearly, willingly adopted certain qualities that Tom also suffered, like his difficulty—no, his inability—to allow anyone to get very close. The more I tried to help Kent, the more he distanced himself. It was so awful watching the same behavior. I told him, 'Look, you're my son, I love you unconditionally.' But Kent was so afraid that by then he couldn't even accept love from anyone, not even his grandparents. He'd have a wonderful dinner with them, then he'd get up and say something hurtful and just storm out of their house. My mother and father couldn't understand it. It was just not normal."

The world was radically changing for Mollie and for her family. Twenty years before she had begun a relationship with a bright, talented man who rapidly became a successful entrepreneur. Over time, as he became more and more withdrawn, he became a stranger to her. The divorce was almost anticlimactic compared to the schizophrenia that affected him, and now his son. Kent was now equally suspicious, distrustful, and unable to give any support or to tolerate intimacy. Mollie's oldest son, a brilliant, sensitive boy, was withdrawing into a world from which he would not return alive. She felt helpless, looking for some hope that what she saw might change. The situation was growing worse daily, never improving.

At my next meeting with Mollie, she described the steps in Kent's deterioration, which in retrospect seemed more ominous than she had thought at the time. As his schizophrenia became more and more crippling, Kent became more isolated over the next months and less capable of maintaining interest in and succeeding at school.

"People who had thought the world of him no longer knew him. It was so sad. He was lonely even though he was surrounded by adults, by teachers, and by a lot of dropouts like himself. He worked at odd jobs, and his father gave him lots of money to live on. He traveled to Europe. He said he was going to have to 'fulfill' himself and meet this poet and that poet. He met some very interesting people . . . but he really didn't belong anywhere."

Mollie tried to get him help and even found a less conventional psychiatrist—someone "counter-culture," whom she thought Kent might relate to more readily. But every time the psychiatrist felt he was getting somewhere, Kent would break the appointments. Finally, Kent didn't even bother with pretense, refusing mental health help altogether.

While Kent was no longer attending school or working consistently, he continued to write. He applied for and received a grant from the government to help young emerging poets. Mollie was not pleased because it allowed him to remain isolated. "His strength was never from inside himself. He would come across as very arrogant, really obnoxious, but really, he was just suffering, never knowing how to act with other kids. He never played like other kids. Toys didn't really interest him. He thought they were 'silly.' He thought the kids in his class were 'silly.' Boys didn't like him because he wasn't athletic. Girls thought he was too weird. When he was little I thought he would change when he had more contact with other kids. Now I realize that from the very beginning he was difficult, set in his ways. He was unusual. Maybe because he was such a genius."

Isolation from other children is common in many young people who eventually become schizophrenic. Kent's severe, unremitting, and progressive isolation, even at such a young age, was a hint of later schizophrenia. Kids like Kent do not bond in the usual ways. But this also happens with exceptionally talented, bright, or eccentric people. And the combination of schizophrenia and genius can be lethal: *Between 10 and 15 percent of highly intelligent, formerly high-functioning schizophrenics eventually kill themselves.* Their awareness of their deterioration and their despair for their own future make them want to end their lives. For them, insight can be fatal. To be different from others in some remarkable way, especially in childhood and adolescence, can be a lonely experience. These children think and perhaps say things that make others feel uncomfortable. Or their talent is so unique that no one else can shine. In some particular area, they always win; the other kids always lose. Their weakness is often in sports requiring coordination and in being popular with their peers. The overwhelming and innate desire to be liked, to be loved, to be touched, can lead to despair if they can't find someone who truly understands them. Sometimes they may be "touchy"—a sensitivity that goes beyond a lack of understanding of others.

Depression may be an early symptom of schizophrenia. Young people who are depressed and schizophrenic may become drug addicts or turn to alcohol to numb their pain. Many of the young "street people" we so commonly see in urban settings are really schizophrenic, suspicious, isolated people. It is hard to imagine that once they could have been brilliant scholars, poets, or artists. But it is true.

Children like Kent need special supports to tolerate their pain, and they need close relationships with people who can recognize their strengths and support them when they are in crisis, when just listening isn't enough. As his illness evolved, Kent became less able to allow even those who cared for him very much into his world, including his mother and his grandparents. Eventually, even the limited relationship he had with his father deteriorated. He had such violent arguments with his father that living together became impossible. His moods took wide swings—but then, so do those of many other adolescents. How did he differ from other teens who have mood swings, who act irrational, unpredictable? To Mollie, Kent did not seem as disturbed as the other people she had seen in the private hospital from which he fled. Indeed, she felt that being in such a disturbing environment may have made him even worse, further diminishing whatever remnant of self-esteem remained. Mollie herself had had all she could do at this time trying to raise his three siblings, let alone respond to the child whom she feared she had already lost.

Kent died at age nineteen, after years, not months, of personal pain, a pain felt by those closest to him. By the time he killed himself, most of his family had already despaired of his ever getting better. One month before his death, he made an unsuccessful suicide attempt. This is not unusual. While most people who attempt suicide are not successful, the majority of those who do succeed have made a previous attempt. In Kent's case, he tried to cut his throat with a razor. When his mother was called by hospital personnel, she wanted to go to him immediately, but she was informed that Kent did not want to see her and that her presence would only aggravate him. After his discharge she tried to speak to the psychiatrist, who refused any contact unless he obtained Kent's permission.

Mollie didn't know what to do. "It was horrible because I felt that as a parent I had to have some power. I am, I was, his mother, maybe even the only one who hadn't given up on him. So I wrote him a letter. I heard nothing back. I called Kent a week after he attempted and told him that I would like to see him. He didn't want to see me and I had no choice but to respect his wishes. I will always feel enormous guilt that I listened. I can't shake it. He was so irrational, so cruel, that he even threw it up at me later. In one horrible fight he said to me, 'You didn't even bother to come to the hospital.' So I said, 'You wouldn't let me come to the hospital.' 'So when have you ever listened to me before?' But he had said clearly, 'Don't come.' He was punishing me and trying to hurt me, and boy, he did a good job." Mollie began to cry, deep uncontrollable sobs. She put her head down on the arm of the chair and cried for a long time. This picture of Mollie sobbing stayed with me all evening, many hours after she left.

What's the right thing to do when your child says he or she doesn't want to see you? Do you honor the request, assume he or she means it? Or do you follow your instincts? You want to know more; you need to know more. You call the psychiatrist and discover that because of your child's age (over eighteen), any discussion without the patient's permission is in violation of confidentiality. While obviously, if an emergency occurs, you want your child to have some family support, who determines, and based on what information, when that would be appropriate? If the patient is paranoid, delusional, and hostile, as Kent was, is any interaction effective?

Mollie continued: "A month later he jumped off the Fiske Bridge. He left a little note which I've memorized. It says,

> Dear Friends,
> Please have me cremated, the ashes scat-
> tered over Salem Harbor. Of my possessions
> take what you desire. Sing, play music, read
> poetry in my memory. I loved you all.

It was a theatrical type of note, the kind of a thing a poet might leave. He was into Sylvia Plath and other poets who were consumed with death. He identified with them.

"Tom couldn't even bring himself to tell me what happened. My lawyer had to call me to tell me. I haven't talked to Tom since the funeral. You know what's ironic? Three weeks after Kent made the first attempt on his life, Tom went to family court to get permission to take the other kids on a month's vacation. Tom was isolated; he was erratic; but his family money and position in society protected him. He could appear more normal than he actually was. He was fighting for custody, he wanted to take the others on a trip; it was a diversion for him. He didn't have much chance of succeeding. He could fill his weeks in his empty life and harass me with all this, all at the same time. I was so panicked at the thought of what Kent might do while I was alone, and I was so afraid of what Tom would say about me to the other kids, that I fought him tooth and nail. I begged him to stop worrying about the others, to concentrate on Kent, who needed more attention, especially after his suicide attempt, but he wouldn't hear of it. He said, 'Kent's going to be fine. That's why we have doctors. You forget that Kent was fine when he went to Europe last year. He's bored. You never could cope with his brilliance.' I said, 'Where is Kent this week? Have you seen him?' Tom hadn't heard from him in three days. Kent hadn't showed up at his apartment. He had no idea of what this all meant, none. I went to family court on Friday to fight custody. The next day I found out Kent was dead. Isn't that something? His father was fighting me over the kids and at that very moment his first son was already dead, *dead!* I am a compassionate person, but I can never forgive Tom for ignoring Kent's needs. But what can I say? I wasn't there for him either."

When we next met, Mollie and I struggled together to see if there were any warning signs prior to Kent's first suicide attempt. An ongoing goal of our study has been to isolate clues to suicide, so that we can learn how to better prevent the needless loss of life. A common finding is that the individual who committed suicide knew someone else who had suffered self-inflicted death: a relative, a friend, or perhaps only someone whose story was told in the media. While most suicides can be explained by psychiatric illness, there are usually other factors, like a family history of suicide or knowing someone who died by suicide.

Mollie recalled, "You're right, you know. I've thought about that. A friend of his—some poet who Kent had been with in Europe—died. The other kids said that when they came to his father's apartment one Saturday, Kent was crying hysterically and told them a friend of his had committed suicide. Kent was very distraught. Yes, I do think the idea had entered his mind then. That weekend he talked about suicide with his sister and brother, with his dad, but they saw it as a normal reaction to his friend's death. He never said he would do it himself."

Mollie talked further about Kent's early developmental years, how she would try to rationalize his eccentricity. She never thought of his differences as being mental illness. He was a loner and did not really bond with other children, but he *was* exceptionally bright, creative beyond his years. Because of that, she would dismiss her own inner voices that said he was too different, even bizarre.

Most striking of all was Mollie's strong sense of responsibility for what had happened. I always think that by explaining to someone that depression, like high blood pressure, is a medical illness that needs medical treatment, I can remove blame and help a survivor to feel less responsible. In most instances, suicide is, in fact, an outcome of untreated or treatment-resistant depression, in much the same way a stroke or heart attack may result from untreated or treatment-resistant hypertension. This explanation did not satisfy Mollie, not at all.

She clung tenaciously to her belief that people can fight depression without medical intervention; she was certain there was something she could have done to prevent Kent's death.

I countered with: "If you became depressed, Mollie, what would you feel would be the cause? And how would you treat it?"

"Frankly, I think if I became depressed, I would know that I was giving in to myself, that it was a sign of weakness. I would say to myself, 'You're going to get undepressed, dammit.' " She continued, "Everyone has ups and downs in life. When you get down what's important is whether you give in to it or not. You don't take medicine for every headache. You don't see a doctor for every chest pain. That's how I grew up, and I happen to think it's good. I suppose that's an old-fashioned attitude. That's how I survived the last three years with Tom, and then, when I got divorced, when Kent was in the hospital and I had three other kids to raise, I couldn't give in, could I? Three kids were counting on me. I talked to myself every morning and every night, I wouldn't allow myself to give in. Maybe I have a special gene that allows me to talk myself out of depression. I've had lots of things that could have flattened me in my life, but I'm a survivor to the bitter end."

Mollie managed a half smile, "It's not what you wanted to hear, I know. You're disappointed because you wanted me to accept a genetic theory, right?"

"I'm not here to persuade you about biochemistry. But I would like you to feel less responsible for Kent's choice." The reality that some mental illness, schizophrenia or depression, may be out of a parent's control frightened Mollie.

She continued, "Understand me, I can't begin to deal with causes I can't control. Don't you see, if Kent killed himself and if there was some gene there, something that was passed on to him, is it possible that I or Tom could have also passed it on to my other kids? Last year when my son Shawn got upset about a lot of things, I was terrified. Did he have that gene too? Would he do the same as Kent? I was terrified; I know I shouldn't do that to myself, but I can't help it."

Guilt is painful, but it looms larger than life when you feel personally responsible for events that might have serious consequences. If you learn from it and respond differently in the future, it should be possible to avoid similar outcomes—in this case another child's suicide. If you believe behavior is totally biologically driven and you think you have no basis to feel guilty, then there is no need for you to modify your behavior. If there is no word you didn't say, no time you might have spent, no intervention you didn't try, no special clue you missed, then there is no hope. But if you know that to some extent *you failed* to have special time, didn't seek help or intervene when things were tough, then you can change your responses; you can become more attuned. If genetic predisposition erases the guilt, then where is your contribution? Certainly we can do something differently to protect our other children. Ironically, guilt suggests that if we do things better in the future, the outcomes may also be better. This is a powerful message.

In my meetings with Mollie, I finally understood why so frequently people who have a crisis and feel out of control do not want to give up the guilt. Without guilt over what we might have done, there is no hope that by changing certain behaviors we can prevent another tragedy and make things better in the future.

"I feel more protective of my kids, particularly my youngest, Shawn, who is more volatile, and also very bright and sensitive. I take his moods a little more seriously than I would have if Kent had not killed himself. I'm sure his temper is part of his age. He knows that too, but I won't make the same mistakes I made with Kent. I know I ignored clues about Kent, even when he was little. I must have! His dad is eccentric, so I naturally thought Kent was the same. Maybe it wasn't under my control, maybe it was just circumstances. I know I could have helped, maybe by accepting that something was very wrong with him at a much earlier stage in his life. Maybe I knew and denied it. All I did was chalk it up to his being a genius. I ask myself, did I keep Kent different? I tried. But I still think about the opportunities I may have missed. Why didn't I try even harder? I don't know what I would have said differently but I think I could have stopped his suicide."

A patient whose daughter had killed herself once wrote me that "lost opportunity is life's greatest hell." The theme that there was something that she could have done to save her son's life emerged again and again as the focus in her determination to be more aware of any danger signs for her remaining children. Things can be different . . . and they will be. The more you accept that depression is biological, the more difficult it is to have hope, to feel that intervention might work.

A certain wisdom and humility sometimes come to families after a suicide, as Mollie shared with me, "If you had asked me before this happened if I was a candidate for divorce or a child's suicide, I would have told you 'not a chance in a million.' I was devoted to my family and to my husband. I'm not a bad person, I'm honest, I believe in God. But bad things do happen. Horrible tragedies—young children die of cancer, they get killed by cars, by guns. But killing themselves—in my opinion that's even worse."

More than anything else survivors of a suicide feel out of control. They play the game of "what ifs." What if they had called? What if they had spent more time with him? Or, why didn't I give her more space? What did I say? Or not say? In the process of regaining some sense of control, maintaining relationships with friends and family is critical. The tendency after a suicide is to withdraw, become reclusive. In Mollie's case, she met an old friend who, like herself, was recently divorced. They became friends and then lovers and ultimately married. It is said that when we are in great pain we listen more carefully to both what is said and what is not said. One of the few positive things that some people develop from a life crisis is greater sensitivity to people who make them feel good and a greater intolerance for those who make them feel bad. Mollie seemed to derive both strength and pleasure from this new relationship.

I asked Mollie what words made her feel worse after Kent's suicide. "I would say a comment that suicide results from an illness like pneumonia doesn't help. But of course, you and I have a fundamental disagreement about that. It's irritating to hear that. People don't die from schizophrenia. They kill themselves because of the stupidity of others. You can't tie up a package that easily. Cancer would have been easier to live with. Nobody can really comfort you when your child has killed himself. Even your good friends are trying to second-guess you. That's what keeps you thinking . . . somewhere along the line I should have been wiser. Maybe I didn't have the right knowledge, or maybe I didn't have enough patience. I *know* I had the wrong husband. Maybe, maybe, you can go over it a million times, but it doesn't make any difference because it's over. What's the right thing to say? Tell people to say this: 'You did the best job you could have with this kid.' Nobody said that to me. They meant well, but telling me that he killed himself because of the divorce was not helpful. Nobody knew how to help me go on with my life."

Kent's story, perhaps more than others in this book, illustrates how understanding an illness like schizophrenia or depression might be helpful for some survivors. Mollie was never able to hear it. For many survivors, understanding that psychiatric illness, rather than poor family interactions or other relationships, is responsible for the majority of deaths by suicide relieves the intensity of the "what ifs." Self-blame lessens if it is understood that these are real illnesses that can be treated. But first the symptoms must be recognized or, at the very least, there must be some acceptance that something is drastically wrong. Sometimes certain types of mental illness are resistant even to excellent help. Schizophrenia, which Kent and his dad both had, affected Kent's ability to stay in treatment. Twice he ran away from a private hospital. He terminated therapy with two skilled psychiatrists. We'll never really know whether he ever took his medicine. He was adept at evasion, at lying. No matter how competent a cardiologist may be, some of his or her patients will not be able to be helped by angioplasty, bypass surgery, or medication. They will still overeat, or not exercise, or smoke. They will die.

Guilt gives Mollie Bainbridge hope. If there was something she did not do, she could change her behavior and prevent more pain. Every survivor must find his or her own path to understand the tragedy of self-inflicted death. Others, especially other survivors, can support and help and understand the pain. But each adaptation is unique.

■ ■ ■

Kent's story taught me a number of fundamental lessons. Intelligence and creativity can be both a blessing and a curse. Kent's unusual intellectual talents and gifts isolated him from his peers and obscured the boundaries between eccentricity and schizophrenia. His intelligence enabled him to closely observe his own gradual descent into mental illness and his deteriorating functioning. This awareness of his own madness only heightened his desperation. Individuals with major mental illnesses— schizophrenia, manic-depressive illness, and major depression—require a strongly supportive, knowledgeable family and an accepting social environment. Kent found neither; he rejected both treatment and his mother's attempts to offer him love and support. In the absence of such supports, Kent's mental illness encroached more and more.

How did the obvious and severe family problems affect Kent? Did the divorce, separation, and custody battle make his situation and his illness worse? I would speculate that the most important factor was the absence of available, in-control adults to provide support and direction. Father, because of his own mental health problems, was not available to provide meaningful help for his son; what he provided may have been more destructive than no contact at all. Mother had been rejected; moreover, she felt that Kent's presence was upsetting to the younger children.

Mollie's inability to think of Kent's mental problem as one requiring medication probably interfered with its effective treatment. Mollie misunderstood the cornerstone of treatment for schizophrenia and other major mental illnesses in young people, namely medication.

Mollie's refusal to consider any hereditary factor gave her comfort so that she could live with her guilt around Kent's death and feel in her own mind that she could keep her other children safe. Mollie needed to establish this emotional compromise in order to believe she had some control of her remaining children's future. As incorrect or unhealthy as this belief was, it was unshakable. Any attempt to dissuade her from this assumption only created more defensiveness.

I cannot say whether Kent would be alive today had he received and complied with ongoing medication treatment for his schizophrenia. I regret, though, that his treatment did not include the appropriate medicines.

Ten

THEMES DRAWN FROM SUICIDE NOTES

While doing research for this book I examined and analyzed well over two hundred notes and drawings left by young people who either attempted or completed suicide. Five themes recurred in these notes. Heightened awareness of these themes may prevent some other teen's suicide. With that in mind, let us review the themes.

SELF-BLAME

Rarely did the teenager blame in an indiscriminate or universal manner. Frequently, I read phrases like "if I would have asked for help, you would have given it," "there is no one I blame but myself," and "I blame myself for the drugs I used and the friends I made." The notes left by teens suggest an overpowering sense of *self*-blame, with only a limited understanding or acknowledgment of anyone else's contribution.

Occasionally, young people blame specific individuals and circumstances. One note stands out, "If you want to blame someone, blame Dad." This was a message left by a son to his mother. More often, however, the young people do not blame others but assume complete responsibility for what they are about to do in two ways: First, they often exaggerate or distort some specific shortcoming, difference, or problem they are experiencing. This creates an overwhelming burden that becomes the rationale for choosing suicide as a solution to their problems. Second, teens use such explanations as "my friends treated me badly." The note may reveal that their response to this "bad treatment" was inadequate and ineffectual. Teens may indicate that they could not tolerate the criticisms and judgments of others and were further devalued by their own ineffective responses.

Even in situations in which abuse is known to have occurred, the notes seldom specifically state that the choice to commit suicide results from the abuse. In the minds of suicidal teenagers, their own faults and shortcomings are vivid, and the misdeeds of others are glossed over. In this way they can justify what they are about to do. At the moment that they are meting out justice in their own minds, these young victims choose to ignore the perpetrator and instead sentence themselves to death. They perceive blame in concrete terms, with their own behavior representing the bad, and other people and circumstances contributing only in a minor way.

THE PAIN

Teenagers frequently describe the anguish and suffering they are experiencing immediately prior to their suicide. However, words cannot adequately capture the depth of their despair. They may depict the anguish in drawings, music, and other symbolic forms. At other times, words from favorite songs, passages from the Bible, and religious themes are used to describe their suffering.

In general, the pain is depicted in two different ways: Most frequently, the pain is related to a very specific loss: the breakup of a relationship, being thrown off a team, or some academic failure. It is always striking that teenagers don't say there were many overwhelming losses, humiliations, and disappointments in their lives, but instead pinpoint one particular event. Initially, when reading teenage suicide notes, people react with disbelief: "How could anyone kill themselves over such a trivial event?" Parents and friends will say, "Losing his girlfriend should not have been such a monumental experience; there are so many more fish in the sea." Their responses reflect their disbelief and difficulty in understanding the overwhelming mental pain and anguish these teenagers experience over a specific disappointment. The second way teenagers experience their pain is through intense conflict. It may be with someone loved and admired or an institution or organization in which the teen is involved, such as school, family, or the church. Many gay and lesbian youths, for example, assume, often correctly, they are in desperate conflict with society, their religion, and family members over their gender identity.

The words teens choose reflect the oppressive, all-consuming torment they experience. The anguish has a disintegrating quality to it, so much so that the normally functional and strong individual is barely able to cope with daily routines. Most people dealing with suicidal and depressed teenagers for the first time are surprised by the rapid breakdown of formerly strong and adaptive coping mechanisms. How can someone so young, so inexperienced in life, be derailed so completely in his or her everyday functioning? The fact that teenagers, like adults, can be ravaged by such intense mental pain has been impressed on us over and over.

Teenagers' ability to communicate their distress to others is limited. Boys, in particular, seem to have neither the ability nor the vocabulary to express the pain. Certainly, if it is the first time they have gone through an episode of depression, they are truly bedeviled by a force so powerful that it seems beyond description. The words they choose don't begin to convey the urgency and debilitation characteristic of their suffering.

Teenagers link their pain to earlier depressions and suffering. Suicide notes often trace the first time that the youngster was depressed and actually thought about suicide. Parents are surprised to find that a daughter who committed suicide at seventeen first felt suicidal at age ten or eleven. Their obvious question, then, is "Why didn't we see it then?" The answer is that the teen didn't have the words or, perhaps, she camouflaged her pain so adeptly that it went undetected. Even when the depression and sadness are recognized, they tend to be minimized, misread, or dismissed as typical adolescent moodiness. The enormity of the suffering beneath the surface is almost never perceived.

Most people don't understand the nature of pain typically experienced by teenagers. The pain comes in waves, and then recedes. Although the pain may linger, its intensity is not consistent. It is rare, often only by chance, that adults who work with teenagers are able to interact with them during a particularly brutal wave of depression. This explains why some people claim that when they saw a teenager an hour or two before the youngster expressed profound feelings of sadness and thoughts of suicide, he looked relatively normal and did not speak of any deep feelings of despair. The paradox is that once teenagers decide to take their lives and formulate a definitive plan, a great burden is lifted from their shoulders; as the despair and pain are temporarily relieved, they feel calmer than they have in months, even years. It is exactly at such times that teenagers are most vulnerable for successfully completing suicide.

ADVICE

In the last days or hours of their lives, teenagers make the effort to share both very specific and general advice through their notes, poetry, or art. They may leave directions regarding their funeral, casket, and the clothing they wish to wear at burial. They often direct others on how to dispose of valued possessions or any money they have saved. In rare cases, the suicide note resembles a formal will, directing others on the disposal of personal property.

At other times the advice is more general, specifically asking people to "bear up" and "be strong for the sake" of other survivors. They may advise others on relationships, urging family and friends to "not be consumed" by their suicide but to "go on" with their lives. Sometimes the advice is an attempt to be calming, suggesting to survivors that their lives will indeed continue and that the suicide will not permanently injure them.

If a teen begins to give away treasured possessions, this should be considered an ominous sign. If a teen suddenly offers family members or friends urgent advice on how to conduct their lives it may mean that he or she doesn't expect to be around much longer. In a way, these are deathbed communications. Blame, advice, and direction should be considered the by-products of a mind troubled by a mental illness, not the rational, well-thought-out comments of the loved one during more sane times.

SECRETS

Young people will frequently reveal some aspect of their personality or private life that was not apparent during their lifetime in their suicide note. Whether it was a love that was not reciprocated, a pregnancy, a homosexual desire, or some wrongdoing (either real or imagined), the overwhelming and consuming nature of the secret should be recognized. Indeed, it is likely that the secret controlled the young person's mind and burdened him with unimaginable suffering. If the teen had known how to unburden himself, would he be alive? It is simplistic to suggest that the secret singly and directly led to the suicide. It is accurate, however, to suggest that the secret was one more burden that weighed heavily on a troubled, vulnerable individual. Surprisingly, in a number of instances survivors have acknowledged that they knew the "secret" for some time and that they were not surprised to read it in the suicidal communication. Regrettably, the teenager felt that the survivors were unaware of it and would judge him harshly if they knew. Had the teenager only known, he may have been alive today.

Usually, the secrets merely reflect the teenagers' profound depression. The "misdeeds" or "wrongdoings" were solely a product of a troubled mind and did not really occur. This type of perception is known as a delusional depression. We have seen youngsters who have felt they had murdered someone, were pregnant, had AIDS, or had committed some horrendous crime. These beliefs were more shocking because they were untrue.

REPENTANCE

Almost all suicidal young people convey sorrow not only about the pain that they have caused the survivors but also about the conduct of their lives up to that moment in time. They acknowledge that the suicide will now become an additional burden to those left behind. More important, teenagers are overwhelmed by the burden that they have been to others, especially within the last few weeks and months of their lives. They recognize the disturbing effect they have had on others. They ask to be universally forgiven for what they have done and are about to do.

What is remarkable is that the survivors may feel intense compassion and empathy but rarely, if ever, truly forgive the person who commits suicide; there is too much hurt and anger for forgiveness. The suicidal teenager almost completely misreads the effect that the suicide will have on the survivors. This misperception results from the all-encompassing pain experienced at the time of the suicide. Asking for forgiveness just doesn't work.

■ ■ ■

Talking with families who have lost teenagers to suicide, I have witnessed unimaginable suffering. I continue to be amazed at how parents, siblings, and friends gradually recover, each in his or her own unique way. The teenagers and their families have taught me that there are things missed and never seen, or seen but not fully understood, which result in profound tragedies. I know more now about what to do and what not to do. I am now better prepared to confront young people and their suffering.

PATHWAYS THROUGH PAIN TO SURVIVAL

Parents, siblings, relatives, peers, teachers—all those who have had close contact with the young person who commits suicide—consider themselves survivors of a traumatic life event. For family members recovery is a particularly prolonged and arduous process, charged not only with grief but also with recriminations, doubts, anger, and fear. The intense feelings of the first weeks may abate over time, but they return hauntingly, achingly, poignantly, for what seems like forever. For most others who were acquainted with the individual, feelings of guilt, fear, abandonment, and vulnerability are typical.

There is something innate in humans that enables us to adapt during physical or psychological crises. Often, to our own surprise, we demonstrate unique strength and function superbly under stress. As time passes, however, this inner resolve breaks down and we become consumed with the catastrophe and the loss. For some this occurs suddenly, soon after the crisis; for others the process is more gradual. But it always happens.

In the preceding chapters, we have examined the responses of eight families who have lost a child to suicide. Some parents and siblings have managed, reluctantly, over time, to accept their child's choice as his or hers alone; others will continue to regard the death as the fault of someone—a therapist, a peer, a spouse, or themselves. Whatever their personal resolutions, the memory of the lost child and the circumstances of his or her death are never far from their consciousness.

They may have symptoms of post-traumatic stress disorder, including dreams about the child and the discovery of the suicide, and obsessive rumination over the events leading up to the person's death. Never feeling completely at rest and having trouble sleeping are also common.

More often than not, psychological and physical changes are experienced. Severe physical symptoms may result, generally as a consequence of individuals' attempts to integrate such an unexpected and traumatic event. Changes in family relationships and communication occur. For some families, the suicide becomes the lightning rod that brings them together; for others the death exacerbates long festering problems.

Suicide has many of the characteristics of a stressor that triggers aftershock. The death is generally unexpected. Survivors feel out of control. Someone close to them has died, and they were unable to prevent it. Even if the person had a history of serious depression, the actual time, place, and method of the suicide usually come as a surprise. Nightmares, negative memories of the person who died, intrusive thoughts about how he or she died, and difficulties concentrating—any and all of these may result. An overwhelmingly negative view of life may color all of the survivor's interactions. To make matters worse, the stigma associated with a suicide limits the social support available when it is most needed. Family members, friends, and colleagues may be awkward, uncomfortable, and stilted in their responses. Finally, blame haunts those who survive, influencing their attempts to find out what went wrong, how things might have been different.

Understandably, anxiety and depression are common among survivors. Several studies[1] have shown that marital troubles, work or school related problems, and emotional illness may develop or worsen significantly following a suicide. Physical illnesses, such as diabetes, thyroid disease, ulcers, colitis, high blood pressure, and heart attacks, may be aggravated or occur for the first time in the aftermath of suicide.

Survivors play the game of *"what ifs."* They search frantically for the *"whys."* Like survivor guilt, the "ifs" are a way to seek some control. If something, someone, could be found responsible for the tragedy, if some guilt could be assigned, then some understanding and perhaps acceptance would be possible. The "ifs" and "whys" offer the survivors an illusory understanding of a meaningless tragedy. Nevertheless, the pursuit of answers is futile and often harmful to those who are blamed.

Irritability and intolerance follow in the aftermath of suicide; as a result, some of the most vital relationships are fractured, sometimes irreparably. Marriages and love affairs may end. Families quarrel more. People quit jobs and withdraw from their usual activities and leisure pursuits; they become alienated from their religion. Even if family or community support is available, parents and siblings feel totally alone in their grief. Every suicide has a unique impact on family members, on their circle of friends, and within their community. Anniversaries, holidays, and birthdays become reminders of hurtful memories. Sorting through personal effects, clothing, books, and tapes magnifies the aching.

There may be a ripple effect, a "cluster" of suicides or suicide attempts in the community. Teens have been known to follow suicide pacts among their peers. The suicide of a celebrity can trigger a number of other suicides, and perhaps inadvertently become a behavioral model for self-destruction in vulnerable, hurting teens. Is the notoriety like a germinating seed? Why does one death make another seem like a good idea? Does the media coverage glamorize suicide?

The death of a friend or role model inadvertently gives depressed teens permission to think death may be an acceptable alternative to their problems. They become aware of the attention, the fame, that suicide can bring. I have frequently spoken to journalists about writing about a community or celebrity suicide as a lesson about depression, or gun control, or substance abuse, rather than dwelling on the gory aspects of the actual death.

A less common aftermath is an epidemic of suicides in a short time. Later victims are not always close friends of the first suicide. Only rarely do friends or other family members die to "join" the person in the hereafter. It may be months or years later before a survivor attempts suicide. A time of particular risk is when a surviving child is at the same age as the parent who committed suicide a generation earlier. In many instances, the child suffers the same illness as the parent suffered, usually major depression or manic-depressive illness.

The intensity and duration of the psychological and physical responses to suicide can be allayed by appropriate community, medical, and social resources. Survivor support groups can play a fundamental role in the resolution of grief and pain. But they are only one resource. When distress continues, other steps should be considered: seeking professional medical help, not only for psychological support but also for evaluation of increased risk for health problems and/or depression; making a greater effort to reach out to family and good friends and strengthening those ties; and reassessing individual priorities.

PHYSICAL AND EMOTIONAL REACTIONS TO LOSS

Some survivors' symptoms are partially or completely physical. This is particularly the case when the suicide is not openly discussed. Often, if we cannot address or alleviate psychological suffering, our bodies respond to the stress. Research[2] has shown that a major physical illness can actually be triggered by a suicide; it may even cause the premature death of a survivor. Heart attacks and strokes are commonly cited as examples. I have spoken with a survivor who developed insulin-dependent diabetes six weeks after his sister died of an overdose. Another person who had cancer in remission literally gave up and died of metastases a few weeks after her husband's suicide. It is essential to pay attention to those physical symptoms that may emerge, so that they can be treated immediately.

The chance discovery of something belonging to the child who died can renew the raw emotions connected to the day of the suicide. One mother was cleaning out a kitchen drawer one Saturday morning two years after her son's suicide and discovered a valentine he had sent her ten years earlier. It was as if she had just discovered his body. How could it have happened? Was it really her son who died? What went wrong in his life for him to hurt himself?

There is a finality implicit in disposing of belongings once treasured by someone who has died. In most instances of adolescent suicide, secrets are discovered in diaries, letters, and hidden artwork. Sometimes a mother finds that a daughter she had assumed to be a virgin was pregnant. One mother found entries in her daughter's diary revealing that for years her stepfather had sexually abused her and threatened to kill her if she spoke of the abuse. Parents learn about their child's drug and alcohol experimentation. One father who had attended all his son's football, basketball, and baseball games found out that his son was homosexual. He had his son buried with his football helmet. He refused to recognize his son's lover at the funeral— a young man who was the quarterback on the team his son captained. He stood up at the funeral mass to tell those assembled that his son was not gay. Somehow, the suicide forces others to know the adolescent more honestly and completely than he or she was known in life.

It is natural for survivors to experience some degree of depression. After all, their world is irrevocably changed. Depression forces us to decelerate while we heal. This decreased psychological and physical pace allows our bodies and our minds to recuperate. For some, symptoms may resemble the same depression that afflicted the individual who committed suicide. Mourning is transformed into melancholia. Sleep becomes impossible. There is a loss of appetite, weight loss—or just the opposite, marked overeating and weight gain. Mornings are the worst; the survivor does not want to get out of bed until late in the day. Sexual interest dwindles. The whole world seems to be cast in grays and blacks. The sudden shock to one's system brought on by a suicide turns into a full-blown depression. There may always be a sense of pain and loss, but with time sleep, appetite, energy, and sexual interest gradually improve.

If there is no improvement—or worse yet, if these symptoms become more intense—psychiatric help is advisable. Some survivors are too numb to cry during the acute phase of grief because the disbelief and shock are so great; the numbness persists and they become the walking dead. Others are as tearful two years after the suicide as they were the day it happened. The long-standing depression and ongoing tearfulness have become a habitual pattern of living and may be resistant to treatment.

ISOLATION AND DENIAL

When we lose someone to suicide, all our priorities change. We are tested with the incomprehensible enigma of self-inflicted death. We become more intolerant, irritable, and impatient with petty concerns. We become more alert to what is said, by whom, and to what is not said.

How many people do we know personally, very personally, who have lost someone to suicide? Most of us, especially if we're young, know few, if any. We all know someone who has lost a parent or grandparent to illness; even little children know other children who have lost a parent or grandparent. Most families have relatively easy access to support when they lose a family member through illness or accidental death. The community, the church, neighbors—all find a way to help the bereaved.

Usually there is no such natural support group of family and peer survivors in the case of suicide. Families may have to go miles, maybe even to a national meeting, to find a support network. This isolation is magnified when other family and friends do not accept the suicide, or if they blame the survivors, or if the family for religious or social reasons has to lie about the cause of death. The circle of friends who feel uncomfortable, threatened, or overwhelmed by talking about suicide grows; survivors may become more isolated.

Sometimes survivors are most comfortable spending time alone or with only a few close friends, family members, and other survivors. Gradually, this nucleus of friends, many of whom have worked through a similar grieving process, help the survivor come to terms with the loss, while they also provide support, comfort, and direction. Meeting with those who have experienced the same shock, sadness, and anguished healing process can be very therapeutic.

Awkward questions ("What did your son die from?"), as well as insensitive comments ("I heard your son killed himself. Was he on drugs?"), are sufficient to make a survivor withdraw when he or she feels fragile and vulnerable. The most poignant story we have heard was from a father who, when asked by acquaintances what caused his son's death, replied, "Leukemia." He just couldn't bring himself to be honest. Even as he heard himself lie, he was ashamed and remorseful. The need to hide the truth comes from a number of sources. "I am ashamed and feel responsible for my son's death," one parent said to me, "My punishment for my crimes is to be put in isolation and be alone."

How do parents confront the fact that their own child has made such a terrible choice? Some never do, refusing to avail themselves of the help and support of a survivor group. Denial is a brittle defense, easily fractured. To maintain it, the person who denies must isolate himself or herself from those who speak openly of the suicide. In that way, it is possible to minimize input that makes suicide real, such as attendance at survivor groups or reading books that detail the loss of others. This makes it difficult for those close to them, particularly other family members, to come to terms with the loss. They erect barriers to keep other family members and friends at a distance. In some instances, one spouse accepts the loss while the other does not.

Family members generally vary in how they respond to tragedy and in the time frame needed to adapt. In one family, a mother whose son died by suicide immediately sought solace in a survivor group. Her husband could not understand why she attended such a group. He maintained, "No son of mine would ever kill himself." She could not discuss her feelings with her husband, which led to a growing isolation, and ultimately culminated in separation and divorce. To this day, the husband feels his wife left him because she saw "too many TV shows about suicide." His son "was experimenting with drugs and just took too much." For him, there could be no other explanation.

Suicide is difficult not only for immediate survivors but also for the community. Because of their inability or their discomfort in dealing with the subject of suicide, some people, even close friends, avoid the subject or the survivor. It's almost as if the person never existed. News of a suicide in a community is often fuel for rumors about the victim, the family, even friends or teachers. Just recently, while visiting my childhood home, I heard about a suicide that weekend of a twenty-year-old boy. In the two days I was there I heard at least half a dozen versions of his death and opposing views of his problems. Few were true. Much later I heard that he had been schizophrenic for years and had rejected many efforts at treatment.

When someone dies by suicide, we are all survivors. We all feel it. When individuals avoid survivors or when they are at a loss for words or appear awkward, they are really reflecting the same behavior as survivors who don't want to be asked questions, who are awkward or tongue-tied. One teenage survivor described feeling as though he had leprosy when his brother died. When people did speak with him, they could not be spontaneous. He felt grief, shame, and abandonment. Frequently, it becomes impossible for some friends to treat the parent or sibling as they had before. What they are really reflecting is their own terror. It becomes too difficult to identify with the survivor. After all, it could be their own son or daughter. They can well imagine the pain of the loss of their child. Too frightened to respond to their own emotional reactions, they distance themselves from the survivors. Other friends don't want to talk about their children, their milestones, because it would be too cruel a reminder of what might have been, of what was lost.

Desire for Revenge—Or at Least an Explanation

A desire for revenge is often present, especially if a contributing factor can be identified (rationally or irrationally). "Someone should have been able to save her." "How can there be a good God who could allow this?" "After all those hospitalizations and expensive therapy, this happens! Doctors! Hospitals! They don't care!" "The police should have saved him!" "She was driven to suicide by her classmates—they teased her!"

The anger at the loved one's unfair death by suicide may be expressed in many ways and directions. A specific doctor, doctors in general, bad peer influences, and God are all natural targets. Someone somewhere should be held accountable. Is it God? Is it the doctors? Mother? Who? Counselors, psychiatrists, spouses, siblings, and friends may be suspect. A friend started him or her on street drugs; that did it. The other parent didn't spend enough time with the child. In some situations, blaming leads to acrimony and divorce. "You didn't want him. That's why he did this. Now I don't want you."

Some survivors go to their priest, minister, or rabbi, and "demand" an explanation. Suicide raises considerable concerns regarding religion and the existence of God. Faced with the cruel death of a child, even a believer may question God. There is speculation[3] that the covert basis for public condemnation of suicide by many religions arises from the questions raised about a merciful or unjust God. In some religious traditions, the suicide is seen as an ultimate sin and the survivors are not supported. How can a young person be condemned in that way? How can the church or community turn their back on a grieving family?

For most people, however, solace and comfort can be found in religion and support from those who share communion in their faith. People are sometimes comforted by a belief in an afterlife in which they will see the person they loved again. There will be peace for them in heaven. Ironically, this belief is sometimes a rationale used by younger children who attempt suicide. "I'll see Grandma up in heaven" is something we've heard from more than one child under the age of ten who attempted suicide. A higher rate of suicide is found in children who have a very concrete and fundamentally understood belief in heaven than in those who do not.

FEAR AND WORRIES

Often survivors, usually children, develop profound fears and obsessive worries. They become consumed with the irrational fear that a parent or another sibling will die in the same way. One ten-year-old girl stayed awake at her bedroom window every time her parents went out in the evening. She was afraid that she would never see them again. Her brother had given no warning of his planned suicide; when she returned from a birthday party with her parents one Saturday, the three of them found his body. Her fear was that, like her brother, her parents would die suddenly and unexpectedly. Her anxieties persisted for years. It was a long time before she could trust that those closest to her would not abandon her. In child and adolescent psychiatry we refer to this as separation anxiety—the irrational worry that something bad will happen to loved ones or to oneself when apart.

Panic attacks, like fears, may occur, particularly when an individual has been close to the person and / or discovered the body. One woman, who had heard a gunshot and then, when her son didn't return, went to the garden and found him lying dead, was flooded with anxiety every time she heard anything that sounded remotely like a gunshot or saw someone shot on television or in a movie. Her heart would race. She would have palpitations and would feel an unshakable sense of impending doom.

In some people, fears, panic, and obsessive worrying occur together. Surviving parents may worry continually about whether another child may kill himself or herself. If the child doesn't call for a while, the obsessive worrying may give way to anxiety, anxiety to panic. Although parents may try to reassure themselves that this child is different, their fears may only gradually recede.

NIGHTMARES, FLASHBACKS, AND HALLUCINATIONS

The most traumatic event of the suicide is finding the body. The gruesome details become the anatomy of an eternal nightmare. To minimize the potential for long-term disability survivors must ventilate about what they saw, how they felt at the time, and how they feel now. And what about the last person who spoke to the victim? "Could the suicide have been anticipated?" "Was there some sense of the depression?" "What clue did I miss?" "Did the death occur seconds, minutes, hours, or days later?" "Should I have noticed something?" "Could I have intervened?" These questions all come up again and again.

Survivors commonly experience flashbacks, particularly if they were at the scene of the discovery. They see it all anew: the body, the noose, or blood if a gun or knife was used. The extreme psychic trauma imprints the painful image in the consciousness and is the basis for recurring visions that appear randomly and unexpectedly, out of the person's control.

Frequently, survivors hear the voice of the person who died. Perhaps they hear movement in the room where their child ended his or her life, or they catch a glance in a crowd of someone who resembles the person. Anything that reminds them visually or auditorily of a loved one's presence makes them think they see or hear him or her. It takes time to process that the person is dead, suddenly, gone forever. This knowledge can only gradually be assimilated. Occasionally, this process gets stuck. Surviving parents create a "museum of their child" in their house, never altering the furniture, clothing, or possessions. At times, this is like a "psychological mummification," where the person is preserved emotionally within the context of the family.

SEXUAL DYSFUNCTION

One of the most fragile elements of our emotional being is our ability to have sex. When someone near to us dies, no matter the circumstances, we conserve our resources. Depression, mourning, and preoccupation with the loss contribute to a diminished or absent sexual interest. One survivor said she could not enjoy sex for three years following her son's death. Enjoying sex becomes synonymous with forgetting the pain, the death, the circumstances. Suicide can represent an all-encompassing rejection—physical, emotional, and sexual. It takes time to rebuild one's self-esteem and feel like a willing and desirable partner in lovemaking.

On the other hand, loss of self-respect and devaluation of oneself can lead survivors to a kind of pseudo-intimacy and dependency on a physical but unemotional level. One mother I interviewed, whose husband had left her after their nineteen-year-old son killed himself, began drinking and picking up men. If someone wanted more than a casual relationship, she would refuse to see him again. She wanted to be a "whore" so she would no longer need to feel. She wanted to hurt others as she herself had been hurt by only using them for sex. She was not prepared to commit herself at an emotional level, lest she be hurt by another loss.

ACTING-OUT BEHAVIORS

If a person is genetically predisposed or has a history of substance abuse, the stress of the suicide of a close friend or relative may lead to more drinking and drug use, primarily to dull the pain. For most survivors, though, the substance abuse only makes the depression and emptiness worse. The impairment of judgment and the increased impulsivity that come with intoxication enhance the risk of suicide and other self-destructive behavior. Survivors who turn to drugs and drink need a rapid referral for support and professional help.

Acting-out and antisocial behaviors can take many forms. Teenagers may skip school, steal, commit vandalism, or use drugs. It is common for siblings to do poorly in school, to have problems concentrating, to reject the goals and values their families have espoused. Their argument is, "What's the point? It doesn't matter what I do!" In the midst of mourning and heartache, it becomes an enormous burden to try and respond to other people's needs and demands. At a time when families need to consolidate and regroup, acting-out behavior may go unchecked for too long, precipitating a new cycle of difficulties.

PAINFUL COMPARISONS

Loss by suicide is never truly resolved. It is unnatural for a child to go before "their time." The intensity of the pain, the lack of orderliness, the inability of others to provide support, and the lack of an opportunity for survivors to ventilate contribute to the duration of the grief response.

It is common to ease the pain of a loss by comparing our own troubles with those of others. Sometimes it works. Any comparison of losses works less well as a loss becomes more personal, and least well when the loss is irreplaceable. Then it doesn't work well at all. A woman who just had a mastectomy is not comforted by a well-meaning friend saying, "You're lucky! I know someone who has liver cancer."

When someone we love dies by suicide, there can be no loss so deep. In one survivor group, a woman in her sixties who lost her husband to suicide said, "Nothing can be as painful as losing your spouse like that. Your children don't want to talk about it, or maybe they even blame you. Few people, including good friends, can accept the fact that even people who are successful and physically healthy, with good friends and a supportive family, can commit suicide." A couple who had just lost their son, the valedictorian of his high school class, became visibly upset over this woman's statement. The boy's father protested, "We just lost our son. He was seventeen. Our pain is much worse than yours. He was just beginning his life. Your husband had lived most of his." A college student who lost his mother interrupted, "This talk is awful. I lost my mother, my only mother. I can't imagine a worse pain." Finally, a young woman whose sister had killed herself remarked, "When part of your heart is cut out, it has no name. It may be a husband, wife, mother, father, sister, brother, child, lover, or friend."

There is no rationalizing or equalizing the loss by suicide, not by age, not by circumstance, not by any other standard. Survivors know that nothing can fill the gaping hole created by the suicide.

WHAT WE HAVE LEARNED

Surviving suicide is never easy, but it is possible with support, with time, compassionate direction, and, in some cases, counseling. While there are predictable responses, every case is unique. How we respond is determined genetically, culturally, and by such factors as religion, age, gender, previous experience with loss, and role models of other survivors available to us. The pattern of recovery is unpredictable. Responses such as numbness, denial, or rage, which are often thought to occur shortly after a suicide, may be absent for many months or even years. They may emerge unexpectedly years later. We are unable to identify an orderliness to the reactions to suicide.

Perhaps the most important aspect of providing help to survivors is an attitude of compassionate understanding. Survivors remember the words that brought them the most comfort, as well as those spoken in haste and insensitively. In our eagerness to help we may say things that we regret later. Sensitivity to the survivor's needs and readiness to hear is crucial. Lacking such readiness, the survivor may reject all overtures, in essence saying, "Leave me alone. Unless you've experienced something like this, you don't know what I'm experiencing. Don't pretend to be an understanding, compassionate healer."

In their eagerness to help, some people press literature and facts about suicide on survivors. Others try to reach survivors by describing and expressing profound feelings. Neither approach is completely honest. The best approach is often passivity—a gentle, passive being-there that gives survivors permission to grieve, heal, and recover in their own unique way and at their own pace. If a woman experiences hallucinations, flashbacks, and panic attacks over a ten-month period after the loss of her son, that is both understandable and acceptable; her unique process should be followed and monitored until she has reached the other side in her response to her tragedy. Although survivors share some characteristics, the process of healing is truly unique to each individual survivor. Accepting both the process and its gradual revelation to one and all is our major task in working with those who survive a teenage suicide.

Twelve

WORKING WITH SUICIDAL YOUTH

Statistics[1] show that after a suicide attempt occurs, only one in five young people is directed for counseling and/or assessment, and of this group only 10 percent get adequate and appropriate help to treat their depression or other underlying problems. Clearly, even young people giving us an overt message about their pain are not having their emotional problems met.

More than 70 percent of suicide attempts are almost completely secret, revealed to one or two friends sworn to secrecy or disclosed anonymously in a general survey. Of the remaining 30 percent, those documented in a hospital emergency room, through suicide hotlines, or by police, only a small percentage is ever provided with follow-up care.[2] Research on completed suicide and suicide attempts has shown that adolescents' symptoms are not always typical of clinical depression, but frequently manifest themselves as delinquency, alcohol or drug abuse, or eating disorders, any one of which may coexist with the underlying depression. Depression, which may be the root of the other symptoms, is often not treated until a severe crisis occurs, if then.

There are many reasons why so many teens do not get the

attention they so desperately require; here are some frequently heard explanations:

- The attitude taken by adults that the attempt was "manipulative" or "attention seeking." Too often these youth are sent home from the emergency room or from the police station with an admonition, "Stop acting so selfish, be more considerate. Who do you think you're fooling?"
- A documented and chronic shortage of people knowledgeable about the mental health needs of adolescents, resulting in the general lack of identification of depression and referral for treatment.
- The stigma associated with mental illness that continues to prevent many youngsters who need treatment from going after it.
- The reluctance of many young people to comply with directions regarding getting help. They may refuse to acknowledge that there is a problem and/or to recognize that they need help. This is particularly true for boys, who feel less comfortable than girls in talking about their problems and their feelings. Girls are generally much better at acknowledging when they are in distress, are more accustomed to sharing their fears and feelings with friends, and are more open to seeking professional help.
- The lack of follow-through for those teens who initially receive good help. Often these teens find some rationalization, valid or otherwise, to reject or stop counseling before it can be completely effective.
- Systemic gaps in the availability of appropriate services for those families who lack health insurance altogether or who have minimal coverage for mental health services.
- A dearth of practical, realistic information available about adolescent depression for educators, coaches, parents, and others who spend a great deal of time with students and might notice subtle or precipitous changes in behavior.

Unlike adults, teens, especially boys, are almost always brought to treatment by someone else. Even in this age of encouraging boys to be more expressive, for most it's still not considered masculine to talk about feelings, to reveal anxiety, doubts—these define you as weak and vulnerable. During the high school years (a period in which the suicide rate among boys has risen the most dramatically),[3] dependency and weakness, qualities characteristic of but not exclusive to depression, do not evoke sympathy and support, but derision and doubts about "manhood." No wonder most teenage boys wait so long before getting help, especially if they already have anxieties about their gender identity. Risk-taking behaviors, like driving at excessive speed, drinking, taking drugs, and sexual experimentation, become affirmations of their heterosexuality.

Typically, teens are referred for help by someone else, usually someone they trust: for instance, a friend, guidance counselor, teacher, sibling, or chemical abuse counselor. Peer counseling programs have been successful in many schools, as long as the peer counselors receive extensive training, with emphasis on knowing what resources are available. Peer counselors should refer serious cases to professional resources *immediately*. Parents are seldom as successful as peers in comprehending the severity of the problems and/or persuading their child that a problem exists that must be treated by a professional. Typically, when a parent does bring the child in for help, the youngster may be uncooperative and oppositional, reflecting his or her wish to avoid addressing the problem and ongoing struggle with the parent.

Family doctors, pediatricians, and emergency room doctors rarely have enough training to adequately assess teenagers at risk for depression and suicide. However, other than guidance counselors, school social workers, or school psychologists, these physicians are the ones most likely to encounter teens in the midst of a critical time. *Almost half the teens who kill themselves do so within three to six months of visiting their doctor for some vague medical reason.*[4] Obviously, doctors need to know that a serious depression may be presented initially as a physical ailment and to recognize when and where to refer the depressed adolescent for help.

Throughout this book I have recommended treatment for the

depressed teen. I have also described cases in which treatment was inadequate. What should happen when the teen sees a counselor or therapist? In the pages that follow, I offer some guidance to social workers, counselors, teachers, suicide hotline volunteers, and others who work with depressed and suicidal adolescents.

ENGAGING THE DEPRESSED TEEN IN HELP

Once there is some initial understanding of the problem, and the recommendation is that the adolescent must go to someone else for further help, we must get the teen to agree. Compliance at this point is based on trust in the person recommending help. The professional must also quickly establish a level of trust. If the teen arrives accompanied by someone else, sit down and speak to that person. Get his or her perspective on what has happened. If the person in crisis is willing to speak about the suicide attempt or the problematic thoughts and behaviors that preceded it, let the person go on as long as he or she needs to. Hearing both versions may enable you to filter out some distortions and see if and where the stories overlap.

Distortions are commonly directed at a variety of sources—teachers, parents, or girl/boyfriend. For example, a girl may bring her boyfriend to the emergency room after he's made a suicide attempt. He says he tried to kill himself because she broke up with him and he no longer has a reason to live. She explains that she broke up with him because he'd been acting strangely for a while. He'd been uncommunicative, at times verbally abusive; he appeared to lose interest in her and became more withdrawn. She thought he might even be seeing another girl.

Another common distortion expressed by depressed adolescents is that their parents are too controlling and rigid. After speaking with the parents, we often learn that the conflict is relatively recent and has evolved as a result of radical changes in the adolescent's behavior, like skipping school, failing classes, drug experimentation, insolence, and hostility. A characteristic of depression is that it quickly and effectively alters the perception of events by the person in crisis and those who are reacting to the behaviors.

BEGINNING THE HEALING PROCESS

During initial meetings with a suicidally depressed teenager the room may feel full of anger and fear. These formidable feelings return again and again, and until they are confronted, examined, torn apart, and thoroughly discussed they control the therapeutic interactions and meetings, impeding any progress. Understand these powerful and controlling feelings for what they are and try not to personalize them. Don't consider them as evidence of your inability as a counselor to reach the child. Do not respond in a defensive or equally harsh manner. Comments like, "That was an incredibly stupid thing you tried to do," or, "Don't you see what you are doing to your parents?" intensify the teen's fear and mistrust. It is common for the teenager to "hear" a critical, condemning, and irritated response even when that attitude is not intentionally conveyed.

Achieving a level of trust and openness requires time and sensitivity to the adolescent's needs. Don't hurry the process. Erring on the side of caution, rather than rushing in with advice, could save a life. On the other hand, if your initial impression leads you to believe that the teen is in imminent danger, consider hospitalization, even if this means interfering with the developing relationship.

Trust may develop slowly. One case that I saw involved a sixteen-year-old boy who ever so slowly, bit by bit, told me his story. After nearly ten months of weekly sessions he was comfortable enough to talk openly; together we talked about depression, about how to deal with difficult emotions, concerns about sex and girls, and successful strategies for handling conflict. I was aware, all along, that he was holding back, not being specific enough. Finally, after another four months, he suddenly blurted out a string of risk-taking behaviors involving unprotected homosexual sex that he had engaged in (unbeknownst to anyone) for nearly a year prior to his suicide attempt. He was so ashamed of being gay and so overwhelmed by the thought that he could risk his life so capriciously that he couldn't talk about it earlier.

Admittedly, this boy's degree of withholding represents one end of the spectrum, but the process of engaging depressed people of any age is never easy or brief. Typically, the adolescent has an "approach-avoidance" attitude: "I won't talk to anyone but my best friend, I refuse to see a shrink, I'm not crazy, I'll see a counselor but that one is too far away." They are so conflicted about getting help at all that they take one step forward and then two back. They agree to three sessions of therapy and never show up; they take a prescription for antidepressants but never fill it; the prescription is filled and never used. Some of this noncompliance relates to the teen's need for some control in a world that seems to become darker, more out of control and hopeless each day. The struggle with depression continues over days, weeks, months, and there is no sense of ever gaining control or any capacity to shut off the pain. Suicide becomes an act of control, a means to end the inner pain.

There is never a "quick fix." Meet with the teen in a relaxed and unhurried way. It may take only one hour, or it could take weeks and months to reach a stage where he or she will be comfortable speaking to you. Listen. Watch for nonverbal clues. Develop sensitivity to the unique circumstances and problems that this particular adolescent is experiencing. There is no one formula or recipe that can be applied in each case. Help the teen to regard you as his or her advocate.

Identify the inconsistencies and the illogical jumps in the teen's pronouncements. Encourage and help the teen to verbalize his projections, his excuses, his defenses: "I didn't go for help because my parents wouldn't pay." "I really wasn't going to shoot. Besides, I thought it wasn't loaded." Don't debate the illogic. Don't criticize. Just listen to it, draw the teen out. Don't rush to tell him, "You need to be locked up for your own safety." That only lessens the possibility for disclosure and trust.

Early on, where possible, meet with other key persons in the adolescent's life—parents, siblings, teachers, and guidance counselors. Try and understand any changes in behavior as cumulative over time. Later, as the relationship is more intimate, it becomes more difficult to discuss issues with others.

Ask yourself, what messages is this teen really hearing, and are they being correctly interpreted? He says he took an overdose because he didn't get into his first-choice college or didn't make the varsity basketball team and his parents were counting on it. Are his parents really that disappointed? Do they seem to attach too much importance to these goals or are they being supportive? She cuts her wrists when she suspects she is pregnant. Why does a pregnancy mean no option other than suicide? Are her parents going to throw her out of the house because she was sexually active? Often we learn that the young person has "catastrophized" the crisis—imagining and believing only the worst possible reactions from others.

Show your concern even when the teen is silent or rageful. Never be afraid to speak about how much you care about the teenager and his or her safety. Demonstrate how one intervention on your part can make a difference. This may mean that you arrange a meeting with a teacher who a teen is convinced hates him. Or you may set up a family meeting to talk about how his behavior has affected everyone, how much everyone cares about him. Prepare for the consequences of these meetings. Can these steps make a difference for him? Will they be helpful? If you can demonstrate some measure of success about one issue, you can gain some trust and build from there.

Separate the crisis from any underlying disorder. Frequently, the real crisis is the individual's response that results from the disorder. Deal with the specific problem, whether it's a failed relationship or fighting with parents. "Your girlfriend said she broke up with you because you were acting differently—you put her down, you didn't call her for days. Is that how you remember it?" "Your parents say that all of a sudden you began to skip school, stay out all night, swear at them. They can't understand it. Is that what happened?" These problems are occurring because something else is affecting the young person's functioning.

There are no pills for problems, only for reliable medical diagnoses. If the diagnosis is anxiety, there is medication available; if the diagnosis is depression, a drug from the new generation of antidepressants with very few side effects can be prescribed. New medications and more sophisticated monitoring of schizophrenia, bipolar (manic-depressive) disorder, attention deficit hyperactivity disorder, and other major emotional disorders have all evolved and improved in the last ten years. *But these medications are only effective for the underlying diagnoses.* They are only a *part* of the answer. Medicine will be of limited value in developing problem-solving skills, or in understanding the consequences of illness, or in improving relationships with family members, teachers, and peers. That takes time, a trusting relationship, and solid communication.

It is safe to assume that, no matter how it appears, the attempt probably did not come out of the blue. Look for clues. Some possibilities include a family history of mental illness, a history of abuse, unusual or stressful family dynamics, prior diagnosis or evidence of a psychiatric disorder and/or bizarre behavior long before or in the days or weeks immediately preceding the crisis. Part of your job is to be a detective, assembling the pieces in the puzzle that is depression.

Whatever your role—teacher, doctor, friend, concerned adult—you are also a facilitator, and part of your mandate is to determine what additional community resources are available and can be readily utilized. Is there someone with whom this teenager has a good relationship? A teacher, a best friend, a minister, a parent, or a social worker? Make an effort to link the teen up with one or more of those resources, so that his or her isolation can be reduced. The teen needs to hear healthy messages from a number of sources. The lessons of counseling are truly reinforced by a supportive environment.

Depressed or not, many teenagers we see today are confronted with adult dilemmas and adult choices without the benefit of adult experience. The intensity of their struggle to achieve independence and success is not necessarily matched by their ability to recognize their own conflicts, manage crises, or respond with logical, well-thought-out choices in every situation.

Because teens lack experience they view their current difficulties out of perspective, erroneously emphasizing one aspect and incorrectly ignoring others. This lack of experience interferes with the resolution of their problems.

RISK AND RESCUE

How do you assess the following situation? A fifteen-year-old boy, partying with his friends, suddenly takes out a bottle of Tylenol and swallows a handful. No one knows how many he's actually taken; maybe he doesn't either. His friends who have witnessed this are dumbfounded, terrified. They hurriedly take him to an emergency room to have his stomach pumped. Afterwards, the boy seems unfazed and goes home, claiming that he was "only kidding." "What's the big deal, I only took four or five pills." Is this a legitimate cry for help, is it attention-seeking, or is it manipulative?

Each case is different. Each case demands further exploration. Many teenage boys and girls make suicidal gestures in just this way. Another name for it is "risk and rescue" behavior. In this case, the boy engaged in "low risk" (lethality) "high rescue" behavior. Another, much more dangerous form of this behavior is playing with firearms. One eighteen-year-old boy pulled out a handgun at a party, and then, to the horror of the others in the room, put the barrel of the gun in his mouth as if to shoot. Only he knew that the gun was not loaded.

Children and young teens sometimes act as though they believe they are invincible, impervious to any and all dangers. Some don't think twice about driving a motorcycle without a helmet, carrying a weapon, or driving while intoxicated. It's the same rationale that they use when they have unprotected sex or experiment with street drugs. They have simple explanations for their actions, no matter how risky. But the risk-taking behavior can easily turn very lethal. Recently, a teenager was killed in a game of Russian roulette at a party attended by a group of inebriated teens. The owner of the gun said there was only one bullet and he knew exactly which chamber held it. In fact, there were two bullets, and one killed his best friend.

SOMETIMES WE MISREAD SELF-HARM

When is an attempt not a real act of self-destruction but merely an attention-getting device? We may never know; however, since *even attention-seekers kill themselves,* it may not matter. The question we really should be asking is: Why would anyone have to get attention in such a morbid way? Are these teens expressing a wish to flirt with death any more intensely than a diabetic who refuses her insulin injections? Although every teenager who acts dangerously is not making a suicidal gesture and may not necessarily even be depressed, it is necessary, at the very least, to examine why they are teasing fate in such an obvious way. I always prefer counseling an attention-seeking student over consoling a parent who has just buried a child who committed suicide. Teens who use self-injurious behavior to resolve conflicts or make behavioral statements need to find other ways of expressing and resolving issues.

THE THERAPEUTIC PROCESS

Once an assessment has been made, there are a number of overriding goals. One is to determine whether medication is necessary to treat any underlying psychiatric diagnosis. The choice of medication is always tied to the diagnosis. *There is no one medication to treat suicidal behavior.* Parents and teachers must be open to a number of medication choices, based on a careful and detailed explanation of the underlying psychiatric disorder and its behavioral manifestations. Both the parents and the teenager will be more compliant if they are fully informed of why these decisions are being made. Let parents and teen both know that there are professionals available to them should any problems with medication develop. Parents and child should know about the important and commonly experienced potential side effects. It should also be explained that some medications won't work and may need to be changed, the dosages may need to be adjusted, and blood levels may need to be checked regularly. *For this age group medication is most effective when it is administered in combination with counseling.*

There are new antidepressants that have few side effects and appear to alleviate depression in young people. Many of these medications fall into the class of drugs called selective serotonin reuptake inhibitors (SSRI). The therapeutic benefits are related to their action on the brain's chemical messenger that appears to play a role in most depressions, namely serotonin. These drugs produce a relative increase in the turnover of serotonin to act on areas of the brain that control emotions. These medicines should be used for an appropriate length of time and at the correct dosage. Most antidepressants should be given a six-week trial at the maximum dose before being declared ineffective. For fluoxetine (Prozac) that may be 20 to 40 mg. daily, for sertraline (Zoloft) 100 to 200 mg., for paroxetine (Paxil) 20 to 30 mg. It is essential that the maximum tolerated dose is quickly reached. The person is maintained on this dose for a minimum of four weeks. Antidepressants do not work overnight. Physicians must not be impatient.

The next goal is to approach treatment with all bases covered. The therapist should have extensive knowledge of the scope of school problems, family problems, and any other mitigating circumstances (abuse, drug use, school/learning problems, developmental history, previous medical and mental health histories, and any medications). Where possible, family members, peers, and teachers should be included in the initial evaluation. In some cases, the family circumstances are so problematic and even threatening that consideration needs to be given to alternative placement in a group or foster home. The more information available to the therapist, the greater the likelihood that successful choices and decisions will be made.

The therapist must understand the crisis that precipitated the suicide attempt from the teen's point of view. Was there a loss (girlfriend, boyfriend), punishment (police involvement or parental discipline because of some impulsive illegal activity), humiliation (sexual, verbal, or physical abuse; failing to make the team; poor grades; difficulties with peers)? The crisis must be reexamined from different angles. To anyone else but that boy or girl sitting across from you, the crisis may seem trivial. In his or her mind, though, it has taken on monumental proportions. "De-catastrophize" the issues where possible. Identify the most realistic and promising alternatives.

Determine what strengths and skills the teen had prior to the suicide attempt, as well as those skills that were lacking. The teen may have been a promising athlete, a star student, or a leader among his or her friends. Emphasize, reinforce, and build on those strengths. For some reason, whether it is the depression or some other emotional disorder, the skills that were present before are now compromised, nonfunctional. The activities that were so satisfying no longer give pleasure. What stressors, negative life events, and problems have taken over his or her personality? During the crisis, you are faced with a young person with few working defenses that can be mobilized.

The next and perhaps most obvious question is: Why was suicide the only option that remained? Remember that this is not an intellectual process; debating the teen's conclusions is not helpful. Besides, for some teens, life is truly intolerable. Those who are victimized in profoundly disturbed homes, those who don't even have a real home but live on the streets, those who live in situations of profound neglect, physical or sexual abuse, without any emotional and family support, may feel they have no future. You, as their therapist or merely as a concerned adult, must try to get them first to focus less on the acute situation and then to pay attention to what actions could be taken to lessen their problems. Walk them through the process, step by step. This part of therapy is often referred to as cognitive behavioral therapy. This involves initially planning, directing, and developing a set of actions based on discussions between the therapist and patient together. Next, the adolescent incorporates the words, plans, and actions. They may even rehearse them with their therapist. Eventually, the adolescents can self-direct and guide their subsequent behaviors based on the words and actions taken during the meetings with their therapist.

Even when they can't respond verbally or emotionally to you, they may still understand that you as their therapist may be taking some definitive actions on their behalf and making sense of their unhappy life circumstances. A good example may be for the therapist and the teen to sit down with the guidance counselor at the school and map out some possibilities for more flexible goals and expectations. Stress the need for the guidance counselor to tell the teachers to be patient and sensitive at this time. Meet with parents. Arrange for separate therapy for the parents, if you and the teen both feel it would be beneficial. Work with the teenager to break down isolation and withdrawal, both of which are effective reinforcers of distorted thinking. Withdrawing from those influences that could enhance social contact only intensifies the solitude and the depression.

This stage of therapy can be viewed as interpersonal psychotherapy, which identifies aspects of relationships and interactional patterns that are problematic because of the underlying depression and its associated symptoms. Some therapists only focus on interpersonal communication and skills. With teenagers, we like to start with cognitive behavioral strategies and work toward an interpersonal phase of treatment. Teenagers can look at how they interact with others after they feel more confident in the plans and directions that they have adopted in earlier sessions. It is similar to the quarterback on the high school football team who initially follows the coach's plays verbatim and with time and confidence eventually takes charge of the team on the field.

No matter how flat or sad his or her affect appears, the suicidally depressed adolescent is desperately trying to contain feelings of anger, rage, hatred, and violence. The suicide or the attempt represents the final self-destructive display of this rage. Where previously the rage may have been expressed in antisocial behavior or directed at parents, school (the "system"), or a girl/boyfriend, now it has been turned inward. Not surprisingly, the suicide rate is much higher among runaways, teens in jail, and juvenile delinquents. Don't fear this anger! Allow the adolescent to express it; mobilize the anger rather than permitting it to remain festering inside, growing increasingly poisonous.

Next to anger, pain and hurt are most intensely felt. The hurt that comes with conflict, loss, and depression is viewed as unbearable. The important message to convey to teenagers is that they must let go of the hurt and move on. That should be their focus. Until they can put the pain behind them, they will continue to struggle with how to let go. One of the most destructive forces interfering in the process of letting go is criticism. The criticism needn't come from others; in its most potent form criticism comes from within. The teen's punitive side has already judged him or her harshly for real and imagined wrongdoings. "I deserve to die" is a phrase read too often in suicide notes. Teens who talk about their fear of criticism—from their parents or others—most fear their own harsh self-criticism. The suicidal adolescent is his or her own judge, jury, and executioner rolled into one.

During recovery, then, in those crucial first three or four months, criticism by others is extremely damaging. Issues can be framed differently; instead of "You treated your girlfriend like dirt!" it would be better to ask, "How do you think you changed when you were depressed (and on drugs, etc.)?" Not "You made your parents' life total hell," but, "I guess now you can see how much you mean to your parents. They don't hate you at all." With healing, it is hoped, will come a level of security that allows insight, sometimes painful, always helpful, to emerge.

Impulsivity is another quality that is commonly present in the chain of anger, pain, and suicide. The teen may think of self-harm in reaction to one or a series of problems, but it is the quality of impulsivity that propels him or her to act on it. It is no wonder, then, that impulsive people hurt themselves more often, and that impulsivity is one of the qualities most associated with juvenile delinquency. Impulsivity may be the quality that determines whether people direct their anger outward (homicide, assault) or inward (suicide). Individuals with poor impulse control have an increased risk of suicide.

Often I'm asked the following question: "What about those cases where there is not even one single warning sign, nothing?" I have been told details about a young man who came from a loving family, had everything going for him, and one day just shot himself for no reason that anyone was able to identify. Most research shows that 75 percent of all completed suicides occur on the first attempt, especially in boys.[5] This finding coincides with our information about impulsivity; with increased reflection, some time to think, the option of suicide becomes less appealing. Increasing the likelihood of reflecting longer on troubling issues will presumably diminish the person's suicidality.

WHAT WE HAVE LEARNED

Working with many depressed and suicidal youngsters in the midst of a crisis, I have learned many important lessons. First, I try and make every effort to determine if a psychiatric disorder is present; if it is, I utilize both medical and counseling techniques to deal with the underlying condition. The youngster's difficulties will not quickly evaporate merely because a psychiatric diagnosis has been established. The next step is to address the specific and life-threatening problems with which the adolescent is struggling. These require thoughtful consideration, open and frank discussion, followed by clear deliberate actions. The therapist has to go beyond listening to the teenager ventilate his or her feelings. In fact, ventilation alone can reinforce the negative mood typical of those expressed feelings. The focus of counseling should be supportive, directive, and intent on resolving conflicts and moving on.

Knowledge about the teenager and his or her problems empowers the counselor and other helping adults to be most effective in intervening on his or her behalf. Adults should realize, however, that not all information will be immediately or readily forthcoming, and that only patience and perseverance can ensure the retrieval of some important and helpful facts.

Patience is critical in implementing treatment. The most frequent error in treating depression in young people is not allowing sufficient time for either the medication or the counseling to work. A trial of medication must last *at least six weeks*. Counseling a young person who is depressed and suicidal often requires twelve to fifteen visits spread over three to four months. Regardless of the treatment protocol (counseling or medication and counseling), it frequently takes up to three to four months before some consistent and positive pattern of change can be observed.

The second most common error is to prescribe a less than adequate dosage of the medication. All too often, medications are switched even though the optimal therapeutic dose has never been administered. It is very important for those who are monitoring the treatment of the depressed adolescent to understand the variety and extent of treatments available.

Treatment is rarely simple. As the therapeutic process becomes more intense new difficulties usually arise. When new problems come up, each in turn should be carefully addressed. This is especially true of abuse, either physical or sexual. Specific state laws about reporting abuse must be followed. Confidentiality must be maintained, except when concerns about the youngster's safety, the safety of others, or reporting of abuse interferes with the private relationship being established with the teenager. Through counseling, teens are helped to defend against their role as victim. With insight and more effective interpersonal skills they avoid the role of revictimization. Hopefully, they will not re-create situations that may lead to abuse and painful interactions.

By the end of therapy I often have a great deal of respect and admiration for these adolescents' strength of character. These are young, strong, and vibrant people who have been bowed and hurt by depression. Although it might be easy to be critical of what these depressed teenagers have done during their most dark times, or to react negatively to them as individuals, adults must remain positive and respectful if they hope to help them even minimally. If, as a counselor or teacher, you sense that you simply do not like an adolescent or are repulsed by his or her behavior, end the counseling or advocacy relationship. Adolescents can readily detect insincerity in adults. Keep in mind that attitudes, words, and actions can be healing and can save lives.

NOTES

Preface

[1] Holinger, P. C., & Offer, D. (1982). Prediction of adolescent suicide: A population model. *American Journal of Psychiatry* 139:302–7.

Chapter 1 Teens in Pain

[1] Centers for Disease Control (1985). *Suicide surveillance 1970–1980.* Atlanta: U.S. Department of Health and Human Services, Public Health Service, Violent Epidemiology Branch, Center for Health Promotion and Education.

[2] Garfinkel, B. D. (1986). Major affective disorders in children and adolescents. In G. Winokur & P. Clayton (Eds.), *The medical basis of psychiatry.* Philadelphia: Saunders.

[3] Kandel, D., Raveis, V., & Davies, M. (1991). Suicidal ideation in adolescence: Depression, substance use, and other risk factors. *Journal of Youth and Adolescence* 20:289–309.

[4] McCracken, J. T. (1992). The epidemiology of child and adolescent mood disorders. *Child and Adolescent Psychiatric Clinics of North America* 1(1):53–73. Philadelphia: Saunders.

[5] American Psychiatric Association (1994). *Diagnostic and statistical manual of mental disorders* (DSM-IV). Washington, D.C.: Author.

Chapter 2 Silence: The Mirror of Depression

[1] A list of state parent advocacy groups is available from the Federation for Children with Special Needs, 95 Berkeley Street, Suite 104, Boston, MA 02116 (phone: 617-482-2915; fax: 617-695-2939).

[2] National Headquarters: Compassionate Friends, P.O. Box 3696, Oakbrook, IL 60522-3696 (phone: 708-990-0010).

Chapter 3 "The Push/Pull of Our Relationship"

[1] Approximately 8 percent of eating disordered patients die prematurely within ten years of the diagnosis.

Chapter 6 "It Wasn't Suicide, It Was Murder"

[1] Centers for Disease Control (1985). *Suicide surveillance 1970–1980.* Atlanta: U.S. Department of Health and Human Services, Public Health Service, Violent Epidemiology Branch, Center for Health Promotion and Education.

Chapter 8 "Could We Have Done More?"

[1] Lowenstein, S. R. (1985). Suicidal behavior: Recognition and intervention. *Hospital Practice* 20:52–71.

[2] Shafii, M., Carrigen, S., Whittinghill, J. R., et al. (1985). Psychological autopsy of completed suicide in children and adolescents. *American Journal of Psychiatry* 142:1061–64. Shafii, M., Steltz-Lenarsky, J., McCue Derrick, A., et al. (1988). Comorbidity of mental disorder in the post-mortem diagnosis of completed suicide in children and adolescents. *Journal of Affective Disorders* 15:227–33.

[3] Beck, A. T. (1986). Hopelessness as a predictor of eventual suicide. *Annals of the New York Academy of Sciences* 487:90–96.

Chapter 11 Pathways Through Pain to Survival

[1] Colt, G. H. (1987). The history of the suicide survivor: The mark of Cain. In E. J. Dunne, J. L. McIntosh, & K. Dunne-Maxim (Eds.), *Suicide and its aftermath: Understanding and counseling the survivors* (pp. 3–18). New York: Norton.

[2]Calhoun, L., Selby, J., & Selby, L. (1982). The psychological aftermath of suicide: An analysis of current evidence. *Clinical Psychology Review* 2:409–420. Parkes, C., & Weiss, R. (1983). *Recovery from bereavement*. New York: Basic Books.

[3]Halbwachs, M. (1978). Suicide and homicide. In *The causes of suicide* (H. Goldblatt, tr.) (pp. 192–207). New York: Free Press.

Chapter 12 Working with Suicidal Youth

[1]Sulik, R. L., & Garfinkel, B. D. (1992). Adolescent suicidal behavior: Understanding the breadth of the problem. *Child and Adolescent Psychiatric Clinics of North America* 1(1):197–228. Philadelphia: Saunders.

[2]Garfinkel, B. D., Hoberman, H. M., Sulik, L. R., Walker, J., Sauer, J., & Hawkins, D. M. Adolescent self-destructive behavior (in preparation).

[3]Centers for Disease Control (1985). *Suicide surveillance 1970–1980*. Atlanta: U.S. Department of Health and Human Services, Public Health Service, Violent Epidemiology Branch, Center for Health Promotion and Education.

[4]Clark, D. C., Sommerfeldt, L., Schwarz, M., et al. (1990). Physical recklessness in adolescence. Trait or byproduct of depressive/suicidal states. *Journal of Nervous and Mental Disorders*, 178:423–33.

[5]Hoberman, H. M., & Garfinkel, B. D. (1988). Completed suicide in youth. *Canadian Journal of Psychiatry* 33:494–504.

INDEX

prior suicide attempts made
by, 6, 61–62, 63, 66, 165
schizophrenia diagnosed in,
139–41, 143, 153
sense of responsibility felt by,
40–41, 94, 100, 101–3,
148–53, 154, 168
treatment options explored by,
9–10, 121–26, 136–37, 145
see also families of suicidal
teens; survivors
paroxetine (Paxil), 187
peer counseling programs, 179
perfectionism, 50, 53, 59, 65–66
physical abuse, 6, 88, 100–101
physical appearance, adolescent
concern about, 40, 63–64,
108–9, 111, 113
physical illness, adolescent
depression and, 121, 179
see also eating disorders
Plath, Sylvia, 147
police procedures, 24–25, 26
possessions, distribution of, 7,
35, 47, 59, 147, 158, 159,
166, 172
post-traumatic stress disorder
(PTSD), 129–30, 163
pregnancy, 159, 160, 166, 183
privacy issues, counseling and,
91, 106, 146, 192
Prozac (fluoxetine), 187
psychiatric illness, *see* mental
illness
psychiatric services, expense of,
20
psychiatry, distrust of, 106–8,
109, 110, 116–18
psychoanalysis, 11
PTSD (post-traumatic stress disorder), 129–30, 163

religious belief:
psychiatric treatment vs.,
104–18

of suicide as sin, 92, 170
in suicide case history, 104–18
survivors comforted through,
170–71
repentance, 160
revictimization, 88, 103, 192–93
rigidity, 65–66, 71
risk and rescue phenomenon, 62,
106, 185–86
risk-taking behaviors, 5, 31, 71,
179, 182, 185–86
runaways, 190

schizophrenia:
depression as early symptom
of, 145
early social isolation and, 143–
44
hereditary aspect of, 139–40
high intelligence in combination with, 144–45, 153
medication for, 152, 154, 184
parent-child conflicts and, 139,
140, 141–43, 145, 146
suicide and, 67, 71
treatment compliance for, 144,
152–53, 154, 169
schoolmates, grief counseling for,
22–23, 90–91, 92
secrecy, secrets:
within family, 76–86
suicide notes' revelations of,
159–60
of suicide plan, 7, 177
survivors' discovery of, 166
self-blame:
control concerns related to,
148–51, 154
as theme in suicide notes, 74,
79, 133, 155, 156
self-isolation:
depression intensified by, 17,
31–32, 127–28, 189
in early childhood, 144
schizophrenia and, 143–44